I0279409

Thomas Falkner, William Combe

A description of Patagonia and the adjoining parts of South America

containing an account of the soil, produce, animals, vales, mountains, rivers and

lakes of those countries

Thomas Falkner, William Combe

A description of Patagonia and the adjoining parts of South America
containing an account of the soil, produce, animals, vales, mountains, rivers and lakes of those countries

ISBN/EAN: 9783742896025

Manufactured in Europe, USA, Canada, Australia, Japa

Cover: Foto ©ninafisch / pixelio.de

Manufactured and distributed by brebook publishing software
(www.brebook.com)

Thomas Falkner, William Combe

A description of Patagonia and the adjoining parts of South America

A
DESCRIPTION
OF
PATAGONIA,

AND THE

Adjoining Parts of SOUTH AMERICA:

CONTAINING AN

Account of the Soil, Produce, Animals, Vales, Mountains, Rivers, Lakes, &c. of those Countries;

THE

Religion, Government, Policy, Customs, Dress, Arms, and Language of the INDIAN Inhabitants;

AND SOME

Particulars relating to FALKLAND's ISLANDS.

By THOMAS FALKNER, Who resided near Forty Years in those PARTS.

ILLUSTRATED WITH
A New Map of the Southern Parts of AMERICA, Engraved by Mr. KITCHIN, HYDROGRAPHER to His MAJESTY.

HEREFORD:
Printed by C. PUGH ; and sold by T. Lewis, Ruffell-Street, Covent-Garden, London.

M,DCC,LXXIV.

CONTENTS.

PREFACE.

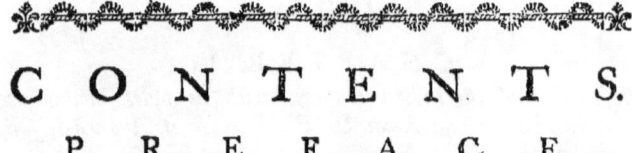 **M** OTIVES to this publication   Page   1
Common interefts of Great Britain and Spain   3
Unhappy diffenfions between them   10
Remarks on the Family Compact   13

INTRODUCTION.

Of the moft fouthern part of America, defcribed in the map.

Account of the map   25
Tall Patagonians   26
Remarks on M. D'Anville's map   *ib.*

CHAPTER I.

Of the foil and produce of the moft fouthern part of America.

Diftrict of St. Jago del Eftero *   29
Travefia, or Defart without water   *ib.*
Produce of the foil   30
Algarrova, and other fruit-trees which grow wild   *ib.*
Quiabrahacho, and other timber trees   34
Fruit-trees cultivated; wine   35
Grain; wax and honey   36
Saltpetre, great quantities; falt country   *ib.*
Cattle and fheep; wild cattle   38
Horfes, wild and tame   39
Gold and Silver mines   40
Medicinal drugs; remarkable cures   41
Tea fhrub   43
Virtues of American tea   45

* This city, which is north of Cordova, is not within the limits of the map.

(ii)

CHAPTER II.

Defcription of the Indian country, with its vales, mountains, rivers, &c.---Great River La Plata, with its branches, fifh, and ports.

Rivers Segundo, Tercero, Quarto, Quinto	46
Mountains of Cordova and Yacanto	47
Fruitful vallies; farms of the Spaniards	*ib.*
Importance of thefe countries to Spain	48
Facility of reducing them	49
Cordillera, or White Mountains	*ib.*
Volcanoes; remarkable eruption	51
Country of Buenos-Ayres, its rivers, lakes, &c.	*ib.*
Uninhabited plains; River Saladillo	53
River La Plata and its branches	54
Bones and fhells of extraordinary fize	*ib.*
Fifh with fcales	57
Fifh without fcales	59
An undefcribed amphibious animal	61
Ports in the River La Plata; Buenos-Ayres	63
Colony of the Sacrament; Bay of Barragan	*ib.*
Ports of Montevideo and Maldonado	64
Northern fide of the River La Plata	65

CHAPTER III.

Continuation of the defcription of the Indian country, with its vales, mountains, rivers, &c.---Tierra del Fuego.—Falkland's Iflands.

Mount of Vivoras and Monte del Tordillo	66
Cape St. Anthony	67
Country of Tuyu, its lakes, rivers, &c.	68
Mountains of Vuulcan and Tandil	72
Sandy Defart; Cafuhati Mountain	73

Country

(iii)

Country of the Diuihets; falt lakes	74
Hueyque Leuvu, or River of Willows	75
Red River, or Firft Defaguadero	76
Lakes of Guanacache	ib.
Black River, or Second Defaguadero	79
Rivers Sanquel, Lolgen, Limee, &c.	80
Lake of Nahuelhuaupi	82
Peninfula of Tehuel-Malal; Bay Sans Fond	83
Expedition to examine the Coaft of Patagonia	84
A new fettlement propofed	85
A facred tree; Defart Coaft	86
Copper ore; River Camarones	87
Country of the Tehuelhets; Anta, a kind of ftag	88
Bezoar Stones	89
Country of the Huilliches; lahual, or alerce tree.	90
Tobacco; Southern Tehuelhets	91
Tierra del Fuego	ib.
Account of Falkland's Iflands	93
Sale of French fettlement there to Spain	95

CHAPTER IV.

An account of the inhabitants of the moft foutbern part of America, defcribed in the map.

Moluches, nation; Picunches, tribe	96
Pehuenches, tribe	97
Huilliches, four tribe	98
Puelches, nation; Taluhets, tribe	99
Diuihets, tribe	100
Chechehets, tribe	101
Tehuelhets, or Patagons, feveral tribes	102
Leuvuches and their Caciques, Cacapol and Cangapol	ib.
Wars with the Spaniards	104
Tehuelhets of the mountains	109

Chulilau-

(iv)

Chulilau-cunnees, Sehuau-cunnees, **Yacana-cunnees**   110
Fabulous accounts of the Cæsares   112

CHAPTER V.

The religion, government, policy, and customs, of the Moluches and Puelches.

Notions of a Deity, creation, and future state   114
Demons, wizards, worship   116
Funeral ceremonies   118
Widows, mourning, and sepulchres   119
Government and Caciques   120
Commander in chief; manner of making war   121
Limited power of the Caciques   122
Marriages; polygamy   124
Condition of the women   125
Management of the children   127
Dress of the men   *ib.*
Arms, offensive and defensive; stone-bowls   129
Dress of the women   131

CHAPTER VI.

An account of the language of the inhabitants of these countries.

Grammatical observations, rules, examples, &c.   132
Specimens of the Moluche tongue   142
Vocabulary   144

PRE-

PREFACE.

THE eftablifhment of an Englifh colony in Falkland's Iflands is faid to be in confequence of an opinion of the late Lord Anfon, who thought that a fettlement, and the fecuring a good harbour for Englifh fhips, in the fouthern feas of America, was a proper meafure for extending the commerce and marine empire of Great Britain. This confideration induced me to imagine, that any information concerning the geography, inhabitants, and other particulars, of the moft fouthern part of the American continent, might be of fome public utility, and might alfo afford fome amufement to the curious. Wherefore, becoming acquainted with a perfon who had refided near forty years in South America, and had been employed in furveying and making charts of the country, I obtained the favour of him to make a map, according to what he had himfelf obferved, and what he had difcovered from the relation of others; to which he added a defcription of the country, and of the Indian inhabitants. He has alfo mentioned fuch particulars of the productions of the country as may be articles of commerce, or were of fervice in his medical profeffion. Some alteration has been made in the language and order of what he had

B   wrote;

(2)

wrote ; but nothing has been added to the narrative of the old traveller.

Another reason for this publication is, that whenever a thorough reconciliation takes place between the courts of London and Madrid, it is probable that English merchants may be again permitted to carry on the slave trade, and perhaps some other branches of commerce in the River of Plate.

The Spaniards having no settlements on the coasts of Africa, where the slaves are bought, have made Assiento contracts ; that is, let as a farm, to merchants of other nations, a contract for supplying Spanish America with African slaves.

The English South Sea Company had an exclusive grant of such a contract from the making of the peace of Utrecht until the war broke out with Spain in the year 1739 ; and the Company had a factory at Buenos-Ayres, from whence the slave trade was carried on much more advantageously, not only with the great provinces of Buenos-Ayres, Paraguay, and Tucuman, but likewise with the kingdoms of Peru and Chili, than it was by Portobello and Panama. The voyage is much shorter; the climate healthier; and provisions better, and in greater plenty; horses and land-carriage are so cheap, that European goods may be sent from Buenos-Ayres to Potosi, and other parts of Peru, at a less expence, and with less hazard, than to Portobello, carried over the isthmus, and re-shipped at Panama for the ports of Peru and Chili. Buenos-Ayres, and the harbours of the River of La Plata, are not only of great importance to the Spaniards in the course of trade, but their empire in South America in great measure depends on their being in possession of those harbours; for their ships going round Cape Horn to Chili and Peru, must in that

long

(3)

long voyage be fupplied with provifions in the River of Plate, or depend upon the Portuguefe, and put into fome port of the Brazils.

As it is probable that Englifh fhips may one day enter the River of Plate, either as friends or enemies, the harbours in that river are defcribed, and an account is given of the fifh that are there taken. A plan of the river would like-wife have been given, but that there is one already pub-lifhed in Charlevoix's Hiftory of Paraguay, in which the foundings were fet down with great accuracy; but altera-tions frequently happen in the fand banks of that river. Since the French and Spanifh Monarchs have entered into their family compact, French trading veffels are often feen in the River of Plate, and other Spanifh American har-bours, and a company of French merchants are faid to have obtained a grant of the Affiento contract. The Englifh may again be the favoured nation in the Spanifh trade, as they were formerly: for of all the commercial treaties, which the court of Spain had agreed to with foreign nations, there were none fo favourable as that of 1676 with the Englifh, as Sir William Godolphin, the minifter employed in making that treaty, afferts in a letter to Lord Arlington.

In order to fhew that there are grounds for the conjec-ture, that, at fome future period of time, the Englifh may be confidered as the moft ufeful and defirable allies of the Spaniards, and on whom they may rely with the greateft fafety, it will be neceffary for me to exceed the bounds of an introductory difcourfe; but the fubject is interefting, and what I offer may give occafion to its being treated in a more ample and better manner.

If the mutual wants, and common interefts, of the fub-jects of Great Britain and of Spain, are confidered in all their

(4)

their different relations to each other, and to other powers, it will appear, that there are no two nations in the world, to whom a perpetual alliance would bring greater and more permanent advantages. The Spaniards are so convinced of the truth of this affertion, that it has long been a proverbial faying among them, *Peace with England and War with all the World*; and Sir William Temple obferves, that the Spaniards, in his time, *placed their hope in England, where their inclination carries them as well as their intereft*. When the Kings of Spain were more powerful than at prefent, and when they were Sovereigns of all, or of a confiderable part of the Netherlands, there might, on the part of the Englifh, be fome objections to a clofe and lafting union with the Spaniards. The vicinity of the Flemifh harbours, and the manufactures and courfe of trade of the Englifh and Flemifh merchants being nearly the fame, were caufes of jealoufy and contention, befides many other political views that no longer exift, fince the Kings of Spain have been deprived of all the Seventeen Provinces of the Low Countries. A miftaken zeal for religion has fometimes prevented advantageous alliances; but that is daily becoming lefs inclined to violent meafures, and lefs connected with the general policy of the ftate.

The many arguments for toleration, publifhed in this and towards the latter end of the laft century, though they have not brought about all the good effects that may hereafter be expected from the moft beneficent principles fupported by the cleareft reafoning, yet they have at leaft fo far had their influence in the councils of Chriftian Princes, that an union in religion feems no longer a motive in forming their treaties, nor will a difference in divine

worfhip

(5)

worſhip be the cauſe of diſcord between nations whoſe political and commercial intereſts coincide.

Trade is an object, to which the powers of Europe give great attention, and which ought to be conſidered as a principal bond of union between the Engliſh and the Spaniards; becauſe the articles of commerce, that is, the over-plus of the produce, of Spain and of the Spaniſh colonies, conſiſts of things that are particularly wanting in Great Britain, or are abſolutely neceſſary for carrying on the Britiſh manufactures, in their preſent degree of perfection. The wine, oil, and fruits of Spain, cannot ſerve in barter for French manufactures, as the French have thoſe commodities of their own growth; and they can be brought to no market in ſuch quantities, and ſo much to the advantage of the Spaniards, as to Great Britain and Ireland. This trade might be extended; as there are many excellent ſorts of wine, made in the interior parts of Spain, which might be exported, if the roads were opened, and ſome inland duties taken off. The Peruvian bark, and many other medicinal drugs, are brought to us only from Spain or Spaniſh America. The wool, ſilk, cotton, cork, indigo, cochineal, logwood, cocoa nut, and other articles, are ſent to England, as far as poſſible, in their firſt growth; ſo that the employment of the artificer, and the profit ariſing from his labour, center in this kingdom.

The Spaniards have hitherto taken more from England and her colonies than the amount of their exports, and the balance has been paid chiefly in ſilver; which ſupplies us with the current ſpecie and the wrought plate, and ſupports the trade of the Eaſt India Company.

It is difficult to gueſs how far the trade may be extended, to the benefit of both nations; for we muſt imagine that, in

C   ſuch

(6)

such a vast country as Spanish America, with such a variety of soils and climates, and in some parts abounding with minerals of every kind, new veins of commerce will frequently be discovered. The salt-petre, and the dried leaves of the tea plant, which are mentioned in this work, may one day be exchanged for British manufactures, instead of draining this kingdom of the silver, with which those commodities are now purchased in Bengal and in China. The exports from hence to Spain are chiefly British manufactures; of which there is scarce any species fabricated in England, Scotland, or Ireland, but what is proper for the Spanish trade.

The present state of agriculture in Spain occasions the inhabitants to be sometimes in want of corn, which has been often sent from England, and with which, from hence forwards, they will probably be supplied from the English North American colonies. The Spanish ships could not be victualled without the provisions that are sent from those colonies and from Ireland. The Spaniards also take from the English great quantities of salted and dried fish; which contributes much to the support of those nurseries of seamen, the Newfoundland and British fisheries.

The course of trade of each nation no where thwarts, or is carried on in opposition to the trade of the other, if we except the contraband trade from Jamaica; which would cease, or be suppressed, as would likewise that of other nations, if the English were favoured in the regular Spanish commerce, and the cargoes sent from Europe, in the galleons, flota, and register ships, were sold in Spanish America considerably cheaper than they are at present. This might easily be done, without diminishing the public revenue of the King of Spain, by altering the present compli-

cated

cated and uncertain mode of taxation, and by abolishing unnecessary formalities, tedious delays, and expensive applications to the Spanish ministers; which encumber the licensed trade, and greatly enhance the price of the merchandize sold in America, and at the same time diminish the value of what is sent back from thence; which would be increased by the quickness of the return, much to the advantage of the Creoles, and of the Spaniards themselves.

Another cause of contention was the right of cutting logwood on the coasts of the Bay of Honduras, which had long been opposed by the Spanish government, but which was given up to the English by an article in the last peace. And discord may have been prevented by a farther concession, likewise obtained in the same treaty; which was, the Spaniards relinquishing all pretensions to the fishery on the banks of Newfoundland. The Biscayners are thought to have been the first mariners who went on that fishery, and if the first possession gave any right, it was transferred by that article to the English.

An attempt to explain minutely every branch of commerce would be tedious to the generality of readers; but, I believe, the more this subject is examined, the more clearly it will appear, that the true commercial interests of the two kingdoms every way agree, or are reconcileable to each other. And nearly the same may be said in regard to the territories belonging to each kingdom; because there is no territory possessed by the one, that can, in good policy, be an object of ambition to the other: for, excepting the rock of Gibraltar, there is not a spot of ground under the dominion of the King of Great Britain, that a patriot King of Spain ought to wish for; and that fortress, and the Island of

Minorca,

(8)

Minorca, might be confidered, more as ftore-houfes for the Mediterranean trade, than as military ftations: or, if they have a hoftile appearance, that may be neceffary, to fecure refpect to the Britifh flag from the Barbary corfairs, and ought not to raife fufpicions of an unfriendly difpofition in the Englifh towards the Spanifh nation. The province of Eaft Florida, which was ceded alfo by the treaty of Paris, in exchange for the Havanna, was of little or no confequence to the Spaniards in time of peace; in cafe of a war with England, that fettlement might have been an annoyance to the Englifh colonies. But, as it adjoins on one fide to Georgia and Carolina, and on the other to Weft Florida, which the French relinquifhed by the fame treaty, it muft have been an eafy conqueft to the Englifh; wherefore the Spaniards, while they wifh for peace with England, cannot regret the lofs of a burthenfome, defencelefs territory.

The river Miffifippi is the moft proper boundary, and the moft likely to prevent all future contefts. The largenefs of the river, and the length of it's courfe, makes it appear, as if formed by nature to fet bounds to the vaft empires of Britifh and Spanifh America. The prefent extenfivenefs of the Englifh colonies will probably delay their defection from the mother country, becaufe it will hinder the eftablifhment of confiderable manufactures; for men will not be inclined to work at the loom or the anvil, for the merchant or wholefale manufacturer, if they can obtain portions of land to be allotted to them, which they may cultivate entirely for their own advantage. The fubjection of thofe colonies to the Sovereign of Great Britain is, in fome refpects, of as much importance to Old Spain, as it is to Old England: for when the Britifh Americans become
independant,

(9)

independant, it will probably induce the inhabitants of the great kingdoms in Spanish America to follow their example; which they will also be forced to do, by their communication with Europe being intercepted; for North America is better provided with timber, and all kinds of naval stores, than any other country in the world. A great maritime power will be formed there, and the people will have that bold, enterprizing spirit, with which free governments generally animate mankind. In such circumstances, the Spanish Creoles must have their commerce with the North Americans. No treasure could with safety be brought to Spain; the galleons and flota could not often escape the North American cruizers, particularly in the windward passage, and the narrow channel between the Bahama islands and the continent. It seems therefore a reasonable conjecture, that an absolute independancy of the North American colonies on the government of Great Britain would, in it's consequences, bring about, in all other parts of America, the same independancy on the other nations of Europe. Such a revolution would be fatal to all Europeans, as it would bring them back to the poverty of their ancestors, and leave in the imaginations of many of them the cravings of modern luxury.

The interests of the British and Spanish nations continue united, both in these distant views, which depend on future contingencies, and likewise in many of their immediate and present relations to the neighbouring states.

France is the power, of which both nations ought to be jealous; an ambitious enterprizing Monarch, like Lewis the XIVth, would be a most dangerous neighbour to both kingdoms. The measures pursued by Oliver Cromwell, and by some of our Kings, which raised France, and sunk

D   the

the power of Spain, are now perceived to have been contrary to the true interefts of the Britifh monarchy. Befides their common danger, to be apprehended from France, the relative grandeur of England, and of Spain, depends on preferving the general balance of power between the ftates of Europe, and the particular balance that fubfifts among the Republics and Princes of Italy. The liberty of the Dutch, of the Swifs, and of the Hanfe Towns, and the remains of the conftitution of the German empire, feem to be objects of great confequence in the fcale of power, according to which the Britifh and Spanifh monarchies are to be confidered.

The harmony, and national union, eftablifhed between them, would be the fafeft barrier againft any ambitious defigns of the court of France; it would have an influence in fettling the trade of the Englifh in Portugal; it might tend to deprefs the infolence of the piratical ftates of Africa, whofe corfairs have often infefted the coafts of Spain; and it might be a kind of bafis, on which the liberty of Europe, that is, the independancy of the different powers, might fafely reft. For if thofe powers are convinced that the Englifh do not defire to make conquefts on the continent of Europe, nor the Spaniards to extend their dominion beyond the Pyrenean mountains, fuch a difinterefted fyftem will give weight to their joint negotiations, and gain the confidence of other nations.

The principal objection to the plan of a lafting alliance may arife from the wars between England and Spain, and the almoft continual hoftile difpofitions that have appeared, ever fince the Princes of the Bourbon family afcended the Spanifh throne. This objection makes it neceffary to explain in what manner thofe wars were brought on; which

was

was by a fyftem of policy, that was foreign and contrary to the true interefts of the Spanifh nation. The fubferviency of the Court of Madrid to the councils, or rather mandates, of the French, ceafed on the death of Lewis XIV, and the Spaniards began to return to a fenfe of their own importance, and their natural jealoufy of powerful and ambitious neighbours: but their Sovereign Philip V, either from falfe ideas of Chriftian perfection, or from weaknefs of body, or mind, gave up the reins of government into the hands of his fecond confort. She was daughter of the Duke of Parma, and, although married to the King of Spain, yet her mind continued all Italian. It is a principal point of Italian patriotifm, to deliver Italy from a foreign yoke, and particularly from the dominion of the Germans; and this the Queen was ambitious of accomplifhing. She had another inducement for undertaking a war in Italy, which perhaps influenced her ftill more powerfully, and this was the providing kingdoms, or independant fovereignties, for all her fons. Thus the ambition of the Italian Princefs, and the fondnefs of the mother, overcame the fenfe of duty of the Queen, who directed the government of a great nation; for the wars were carried on, and the young Princes have been fupported, at a great expence of blood and treafure, without a profpect of advantage to the people of Spain. And as natives might be lefs active and vigilant in projects that were detrimental to their country, the Queen appointed Alberoni, an Italian cardinal; Riperda, a Dutchman; and other foreigners, for her minifters.

The defigns of the Queen were contrary to the political views of the Englifh, and the fyftem of the great alliance formed by King William; but coincided with the intereft of France; not only becaufe, by thefe means, the court

of

(12)

of Spain became united with, and dependant on the French, for the accomplishment of those designs, but likewise, because the settlements on the Spanish Princes were to be made by driving the Austrians out of Italy. So by entering into the views of the Queen of Spain, the French gained a rich ally, and at the same time weakened a powerful rival.

On the death of Philip V, the thoughts of making conquests in Italy were at an end; for his son by his first Queen, Ferdinand VI, who succeeded him, loved the Spanish nation, seldom spoke any other language but the Spanish, and employed none but Spanish ministers. As King Ferdinand had no children, the Dowager Queen, whose sons were to succeed to him, had a strong party in the court; but neither her influence, nor all the French intrigues, could bring him into the war against England; though they might prevent that union with the English, to which a discerning and truly patriotic King of Spain will always be inclined.

Ferdinand VI dying without issue, the kingdom of Spain devolved to the Queen Dowager's eldest son, Don Carlos, then King of Naples. He was, by former transactions, already disposed to join in the French interests; but the ministry of Versailles proposed binding him in a still closer union with France, and, for this purpose, they are thought to have set before him the prospect of himself or his descendants succeeding to the French monarchy, on failure of male issue of the elder branch of the Bourbon family. The late Dauphin was then in a very infirm state of health, and his sons were represented by Dr. Tronchin, as it is said, and the French physicians, as persons of a weakly constitution, not likely to live, or to leave posterity.

(13)

rity. On this a Family Compact was agreed upon between the two Monarchs; by the secret articles of which it is supposed to have been stipulated, that the Spanish branch of the House of Bourbon should succeed to the Crown of France, for want of male descendants of Lewis XV. The name of Family Compact, given to the treaty, indicates some regulations in regard to family successions, and would be an improper title, if there were no other articles in the treaty, but those which have been announced to the public. The reason of the articles which relate to the succession being kept secret is very obvious; because they are a violation of the treaty of Utrecht; in which Philip V renounced, in the clearest manner, for himself and his descendants, all future claims and pretensions to the kingdom of France. The French minister, Mr. De Torcy, endeavoured to evade that absolute renunciation, as may be seen in his letters to Lord Bolingbroke; but the English ministry insisted upon it; and indeed it was the most important point that was obtained by all the successes in Queen Anne's war, which was undertaken to prevent the dependancy of Spain on the Court of France; whereas the intent of both the secret, and the avowed articles, of the Family Compact, is to establish that dependancy.

That there are secret articles, relating to the Bourbon Family, may be inferred, not only from the title of the treaty, but likewise from those articles that have been made public; because the two Sovereigns declare no other motives in those public articles, but their mutual regard for each other, and for the honour of their family; motives, which can only relate to themselves, and not to the commerce or mutual naturalization of their subjects. For it would be too humiliating to mankind, and debasing the dignity of

E   human

(14)

human nature, to suppose that no attention is to be given by Princes to the well-being of the people they govern, or that the lives and fortunes of millions are of no other consequence in the estimation of their Sovereigns, than as they contribute to the grandeur of a Monarch, and the glory of a Royal Family: and I am willing to imagine, that some thoughts concerning the happiness of their subjects are expressed in the secret parts of the treaty.

The two Monarchs had an example of the inordinate desire of family greatness in their ancestor Lewis XIV; who, after the death of the last King of Spain of the House of Austria, was advised by his council to abide by the dispositions made in the partition treaty, and which would have been much more advantageous to the French nation, than to have acquired for Lewis's grandson, the Duke of Anjou, the whole succession of the Spanish monarchy, under the will of the then late departed King of Spain; but Lewis determined on what he thought more glorious for his family, though it involved Europe in a long and bloody war, which brought his own kingdom to the brink of ruin. This sentiment was so prevalent in the mind of the French Monarch, that he alleged in a manner no other motive but his own glory, for the war against Holland in 1672. And he was offended at one of his subjects, who, in some public harangue, spoke to him about the interests of France, and the well-being of the state; because it was his will and pleasure, that Frenchmen should have no other political principles but an enthusiastic zeal for the glory of their Sovereign. The Englishman's love of his country, and loyalty to his King, are founded on more rational principles, and more honourable to human nature. Those two duties are happily united, by our having a Sovereign, who has

no

(15)

no interests that are distinct from those of the British nation, and whose family connections engage him in no wars or treaties that are prejudicial to his subjects, but who considers the peace and happiness of all his people as the sole end and glory of his reign.

Preparations were made for the Family Compact, by the French King's giving up the pretensions of his son-in-law, Don Philip, and of his grandson, the present Duke of Parma, to the kingdoms of Naples and Sicily. The eventual succession to those kingdoms was settled on them by the treaty of Aix-la-Chapelle, upon the contingency of Don Carlos, the then King of Naples, becoming King of Spain; but the French consented, that the Spanish Monarch might deprive his own brother of that succession, and afterwards his nephew (whose mother was daughter to the present King of France), and settle the kingdoms of Naples and Sicily on his third son.

In order the more to cement the union proposed to be established by the Family Compact, and that the French Court might give farther proofs of sincerity to the King of Spain, the Duke of Orleans, who is next in succession to the crown if the Spanish branch is excluded, and the other Princes of the blood, were deprived of that share, or influence in the French government, to which, by their birth, and by the custom or constitution of the kingdom, they have been generally understood to be entitled. The lowering the dignity and importance of those Princes in the opinion of the people of France may be considered as a part of the system of the Family Compact; and perhaps for the same motives the parliaments, or great courts of judicature, have been dissolved, and the patriotic lawyers banished or imprisoned; as such persons may be thought

to

(16)

to be inclined to maintain the validity of Philip V's renunciation, and likewise the spirit and intent of the Salic
Law, which means to exclude foreign Princes from inheriting the Crown of France.

The Spanish Monarch has, in like manner, banished or
disgraced all those who were thought to disapprove of the
Family Compact, and French spies are employed in
most of the considerable towns of Spain, to watch the
disaffected to this new projected union with France.
These proceedings seem to resemble the conduct of
Augustus, Anthony, and Lepidus; who gave up their private friendships, and sacrificed their particular connections,
to the system of the compact of the Roman Triumvirate.
The King of Spain has gone much farther; for he has made
a kind of holocaust, or whole burnt-offering, of all the
interests of the Spanish nation, at the shrine of family
ambition. He joined the French in the war against England,
and ruined his army in Portugal; his fleet was destroyed
at the Havanna; and, after the taking of that place, all
Spanish America lay in a manner open, and almost de-
fenceless, to the conquering fleets and armies of Britain.

Besides these involuntary losses, the Spaniards were, in
consequence of the Family Compact, to lose their independancy, their customs, their manners, their language,
their dress, and become Frenchmen; in order that their
Sovereign might be looked upon as a native of France,
and be acceptable to the French nation. Moreover the
Spaniards, in a course of years, must, according to this
plan, lose their trade and their wealth. For the trade and
wealth of Spain, and Spanish America, being equally
open to the French as to the Spaniards themselves, the
French,

(17)

French, being more numerous, more active and industrious, as well as more supple and insinuating, will, in time, monopolize the Spanish commerce, to the great disadvantage of Spain, and of all the trading nations of Europe, who have hitherto sent their manufactures, and had a share in the Spanish trade. The French will want few manufactures, but their own, for supplying the consumption in Spain and Spanish America ; or they will have East India goods sent from Manilla, in greater quantities than at present, rather than let their European neighbours come in for a part of the wealth of the Spanish West Indies.

By some late edicts of the King of Spain, the sale of wool and of raw silk is so restrained, that the whole trade in those important articles may soon be monopolized by French factors ; and, what is astonishing, the manufactures of Spain are discouraged by the government, if they interfere with those of France. These are some of the effects of the Family Compact ; some others may be less perceptible at present, on account of the disorder in the French finances, and the ambitious enterprizes of the Northern Powers. It is difficult to form reasonable conjectures of what may be the future consequences of this extraordinary treaty ; because there are but few treaties or transactions, in the history of former times, to which the Family Compact has any resemblance.

The public articles of the Compact, in as much as they provide for the mutual naturalization of the subjects of both kingdoms, and the unnatural coalition of the power and interests of the two nations, which in themselves are very opposite, seem to indicate a latent design, that the two kingdoms should be governed by one Sovereign, if the succession to both should devolve on the same person. If

F   we

we contemplate the articles on another fide, and as they announce no other motives for this convention but the private affections of the two Monarchs for each other, and for the honour of their family, they are plainly taken from the fyftem of Eaftern defpotifm; according to which, the fubjects, and all that belongs to them, are confidered as the mere property of the Sovereign. And indeed fuch a vaft empire would arife from the union of France and Spain under one Sovereign, as, in the opinion of the author of the Spirit of Laws, would require that kind of arbitrary government, under which there are no intermediate powers; fuch as the immunities of the clergy, the privileges of the nobility, and the franchifes of different orders of citizens; all which, according to that fyftem, muft be annihilated, and all power and honours made to depend on the abfolute and immediate will of the defpot. Mr. Montefquieu has forewarned his countrymen againft this revolution in their government, and againft the defire of greatly extending the dominion of their Sovereign; which, he has foretold, would be the caufe of fuch a change in the conftitution of the French monarchy.

The plan alfo of the feeret articles of the Family Compact, on the hopes given to the Spanifh Royal Family of one day fucceeding to the Crown of France, was probably taken from Eaftern notions, and from a fimilar piece of policy of the Turkifh Emperors; who have brought, and long retained, the Crim Tartary, in a ftate of vaffallage, by a Family Compact with the Cham or Sovereign of that country; by which it was agreed, as Mr. Knowles informs us in his Hiftory of the Turks, *that the Turkifh empire, for want of heirs male of the Othman family, is affured, and as it were entailed, unto the Tartar Cham.* The Turkifh Sultan

and

(19)

and the Tartar Cham being defcended from one common anceftor, the Cham looks upon the Sultan as his Chief, or the head of his family, and by primogeniture inheriting the rights of fatherhood from their patriarch or firft parent.

There is nothing that has contributed more to mifguide both kings and fubjects, in their ideas of civil government, than confounding the duties of the child with the duties of the fubject, by a fancied allufion between the power of the father and the power of the magiftrate. For as all right and property is underftood to be in the father, and the child has only the ufe of what the father allots for his fuftenance ; fo, according to thefe principles, it is contended, that the Sovereign is the fole proprietor, and that the fubject has only what the civilians call the *ufus fructus*, during the will and pleafure of the patriarchal magiftrate.

From thefe mifconceived notions are derived the Family Compacts, and all thofe treaties which are contracted on other motives than the well-being of the people. The Othman Family Compact has long rendered the Crimea and the Crim Tartary dependant on the Turkifh Emperor; but yet it may happen that the Bourbon Family Compact may not be attended with the fame confequences in regard to Spain, as the wealth, the fituation, and other circum-ftances, of the Spanifh and Tartar nations, are very dif-ferent. The Spaniards have already refifted againft one badge of flavery, the wearing the French drefs; and there are many events that may fruftrate the intent of the French Family Compact. The three fons of the late Dauphin are alive, notwithftanding the prognoftics of the phyficians. If they have male iffue, it may throw the profpect of inhe-riting the kingdom of France at fuch a diftance, as to be no longer an object of attention to the Princes of the Spanifh

Royal

(20)

Royal family. Moreover, they may difcover, that the will of Kings, however irrefiftible in their life-time, is often fet afide after their death; and that the law of fucceffion to the kingdom of France, eftablifhed by the prefent Monarch, may be as little regarded as the laft will of Lewis XIV.

The neighbouring Powers would, for many reafons, oppofe the folemn and public renunciation, made in the treaty of Utrecht, being annulled by a fecret convention. The French, on many occafions, have been remarkable for their averfion to be governed by foreigners; which has been prevented, in regard to the fucceffion to the Crown, by their Salic law. It is true, the letter of that law only excludes females from inheriting the kingdom, but the reafon of it, or the true caufe for continuing that antient regulation down to the prefent time, feems to be, becaufe the Princeffes marry into foreign families, and their children would be ftrangers to the genius and manners of the French nation; which, in the perfon of their Sovereign, would be very difagreeable to them. It cannot be for any fuppofed imbecility in the fex; becaufe the Dowager Queens have governed during the minority of their fons, and there are few Courts where the women have had greater influence. The males alfo have been excluded, who claimed in the right of females, as was the cafe of our King Edward the Third. The oftenfible or law-reafon given was, that as the Queen his mother could have no right, fhe could tranfmit none to her fon; but the true reafon feems to have been, that he was confidered as an alien by the generality of the French nation; and the Spanifh Princes would probably meet with the fame oppofition in the minds of the people. It may alfo happen, that, if the prefent King of
Spain

(21)

Spain is not influenced by a view of the many advantages that would accrue to the Spanish monarchy by a lasting alliance with England, still a successor may see his interests in a different light; or he may be swayed by the sentiments of the most discerning part of his subjects: for the councils of the Sovereign, even in the most absolute governments, are sooner or later affected by the general sense of the nation.

This is the principal reason for addressing the public on this subject; because the merchants and others, who have an intercourse with the Spaniards, may have frequent opportunities of suggesting what is here alleged, and many other motives that may occur to them, for fixing a kind of national complaisance and good understanding between people who can become so many ways benefactors to each other. If unfortunately a war should break out, in pursuance of the scheme formed by the Family Compact, still the good will of the Spaniards might be cultivated, by compassion shewn to those who may be conquered or made prisoners, and by other acts of humanity, to which Englishmen are often well disposed. We might also represent to the Spaniards, that it was against the King, not against the Spanish nation, that we carried on the war; in a manner somewhat similar to the war of the King of Syria against Ahab King of Israel. The Syrians were ordered, not to consider the Israelites as their enemies, but to direct their force against Ahab their King, who had been deluded by his false prophets. So we may assure the Spaniards, that we are ever desirous of peace and harmony with them, and that we consider their King, as he seems to consider himself, not as the head and representative of their nation, but as a Prince of the Bourbon family, who inherits the

G   Spanish

Spanish monarchy as a provision made for a younger branch of the Bourbons; or, as the French would exprefs it, *La monarchie d'Espagn n'est que l'apanage d'un cadet de la maison de Bourbon;* but that we have no enmity against the people of Spain, and no ambition to possess any territory they are masters of; that we are sensible that the empires of Peru and Mexico would be our ruin, and the possession of them would probably depopulate our country still more than it has the southern provinces of Spain, as our extensive navigation, and the nature of our government, will not admit of the same restraints against emigrations as are enacted in Spain; from whence no person can go to America without the King's licenfe. We might add, that we expect no subjection or subserviency on the part of Spain, but that each nation might treat according to the dignity of a sovereign and independant state; that we afk for nothing of the Spaniards but their friendship, and a mutual, well-regulated commerce, beneficial to both nations.

The settlements in Falkland's Islands, in Florida, and on the River Missisippi, may be looked upon as precautions against the too apparent intentions of the Family Compact, and the warlike preparations of the Court of Spain. If the English nation and commerce were treated in a friendly manner, and according to that rank, in which a true regard to the interests of the Spanish monarchy ought to place them, the Spaniards might depend upon both the government, and the subjects of Great Britain, contracting sentiments of reciprocal benevolence; and our naval power, which is now a subject of alarm and jealousy, would then be the protection of the vast Spanish American empire.

England

(23)

England has engaged in wars, and ſpent her ſterling millions, on the moſt diſintereſted principles of heroiſm; there can then be no doubt, but that our brave country-men would exert their ſtrength in favour of a nation, from whoſe alliance and commerce they would draw great and perpetual advantages.

INTRO.

INTRODUCTION.

Of the most Southern Part of AMERICA, *described in the* MAP.

DO not purpose to give an account of the kingdom of Chili, as Ovales has given an account of it already; but shall confine myself to those parts I have seen, and to those that are least known in Europe.

The seacoast in the map is, for the most part, taken from Mr. D'Anville's map of South America, as improved by Mr. Bolton; Falkland's Islands, from the latest discoveries; and the Straits of Magellan, from Mr. Bernetti's map, who was chaplain in Mr. Bougainville's squadron.

I have made some alterations in the eastern seacoast, which I viewed in the year 1746; and about Cape St. Anthony, where I lived some years. In the description of the inland country, I have in general followed my own observations; having travelled over great part of it, and traced the situation of places, and their distances, with the rivers, woods, and mountains. Where I could not penetrate, I have had accounts from the native Indians; and from Spanish captives, who had lived many years amongst them, and afterwards obtained their liberty. Among many others, from whom I had my information, was the son of Captain Mansilla, of Buenos-Ayres, who

H

(26)

was fix years prifoner among the Tehuelhets, and who had travelled over the greateft part of their country; and like-wife the great Cacique Cangapol, who refided at Huichin, on the Black River. I have endeavoured to draw his like-nefs, as well as I could by memory. His figure and drefs are reprefented on the map, and thofe of his wife Huennee. This Chief, who was called by the Spaniards the Cacique Bravo, was tall and well-proportioned. He muft have been feven feet and fome inches in height; becaufe, on tiptoe, I could not reach to the top of his head. I was very well acquainted with him, and went fome journeys in his company. I do not recollect ever to have feen an Indian, that was above an inch or two taller than Cangapol. His brother, Saufimian, was but about fix feet high. The Patagonians, or Puelches, are a large bodied people; but I never heard of that gigantic race, which others have men-tioned, though I have feen perfons of all the different tribes of fouthern Indians.

All my own obfervations, and my inquiries of other perfons, oblige me to reprefent the country a great deal broader, from eaft to weft, than it appears in Mr. D'Anville's map; which I am not able to reconcile to the relations of the Indians, nor to what I obferved myfelf, with refpect to the diftances of places. Even in the Spanifh country, he is I think miftaken, in making the diftance between Cordova and Santa Fe forty leagues lefs than it is in reality. The road is an entire plain, with not fo much as a hillock, between thefe two cities; yet no poftboy will undertake to go it in lefs than four or five days; and the poftboys, in that country, generally travel twenty leagues or more in a day.

The

(27)

The journey between thefe two cities I have myfelf taken four times, as well as between both of them and Buenos-Ayres.

I do not believe that any able perfon has made an obfervation of the longitude in thefe parts, to be depended upon, in order to fix the difference of meridian of thefe places of the fouthern hemifphere. And the miftakes of geographers, in reprefenting this country narrower than it really is, may be owing to the difficulty of keeping a true reckoning in failing round Cape Horn; which is occafioned by the velocity and variety of the currents: A particular account of which may be found in the Englifh tranflation of Don Ulloa's Voyage to South America, vol. II. b. iii. c. 2.

C H A P.

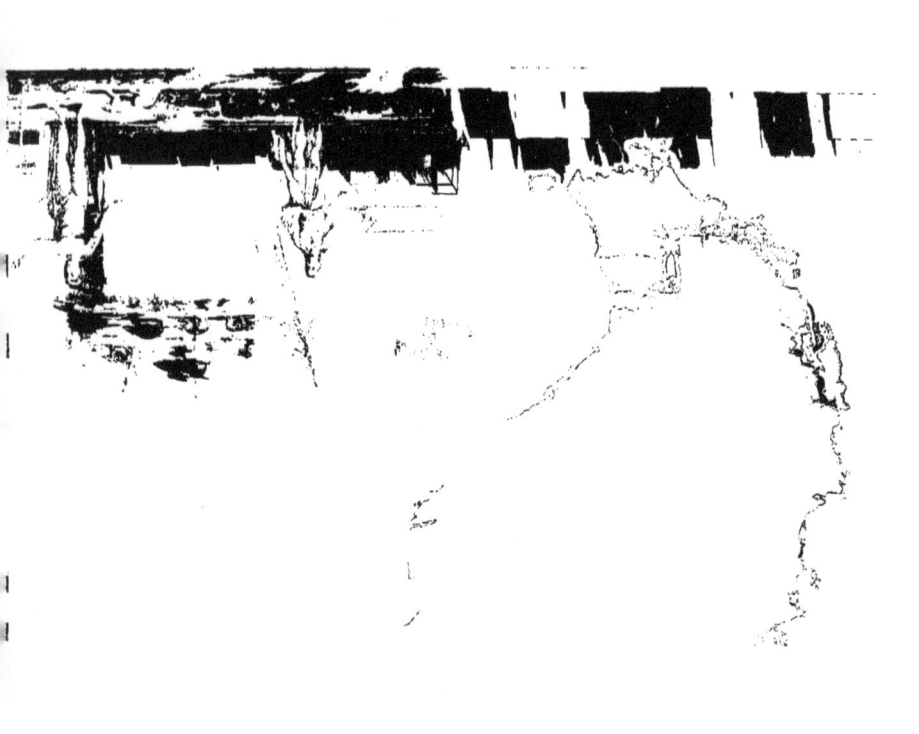

CHAPTER I.

Of the Soil and Produce of the moſt ſouthern Part of
AMERICA.

THE diſtrict of the city of St. Jago del Eſtero, in the province of Tucuman, is a flat, dry, ſandy ſoil. The greateſt part of it is covered with thick woods, which begin at fifty leagues to the ſouth, and reach to the diſtrict of Tucuman, which is thirty leagues to the north of St. Jago. They extend to the eaſtward of the Rio Dulce, near twenty miles, and, to the weſtward, as far as the Chaco, which is above ſixty miles.

There are ſo few open ſpots in this diſtrict, and thoſe which are open ſo frequently overflowed by the rivers Dulce and Salado (the ſweet and ſalt rivers) that the inhabitants are obliged to fell the woods, to get ſufficient ſpace to ſow their chacras. Behind the woods, to the eaſtward, towards the mountains of the Rioia, and thoſe of the vale of Catamarca, are vaſt plains, where there is plenty of paſture, but without any freſh water whatſoever, except what is collected in lakes in rainy ſeaſons; and when theſe fail, there is great danger of periſhing with thirſt, in travelling over them. The great number of croſſes which have been erected, and are now to be ſeen in theſe plains, are proofs,

I

(30)

how many have fallen a prey to their rafhnefs, in venturing upon fo hazardous a journey. This vaft country extends to near eighty leagues, from the mountains of Cordova to thofe of the vale of Catamarca, and is called the Travefia of Quilino and Ambergafta.

Notwithftanding thefe difadvantages, the foil is not unfruitful, when duly cultivated, and produces water and mufk melons, of a prodigious fize, and the beft flavoured of any that grow in thefe countries. Thofe of Tucuman are larger, but, from the extreme moiftnefs of the foil, are not fo well tafted. Corn is alfo raifed here in great quantities, and fent to Cordova and Buenos-Ayres. Cotton thrives very well ; and indigo was formerly a great commodity in this country, but, through the neglect of the inhabitants, is entirely loft. A fmall quantity of cochineal is gathered from a kind of low, thorny opuntia, that fpreads itfelf upon the ground, and grows wild in the woods; and much more might be taken, if it was cultivated, and prepared in the fame manner as in Quito, and other parts of Peru. The foil, with due care and cultivation, will alfo produce peaches, figs, and dates.

The fruits which grow wild are the algarrova, the miftol, the channar, and the molie ; with fome others of leffer note.

The algarrova is a large tree in this country, about the bignefs of a middle-fized oak. It's timber is ftrong, durable, and largely grained. It's leaves are fmall and fcalloped; many of them growing together on one common ftalk, near and oppofite to each other ; fo that ten or twenty of them feem to compofe one leaf, as in the fpruce pine. It's flowers are fmall, of a faint white colour, and grow in clufters, like currants, but fmaller and thicker.

Thefe

(31)

These are succeeded by large, long pods, like those of peas, but not so broad. They are of two kinds, white and black; the latter is narrower, but somewhat sweeter. Before it is arrived at maturity, it is green, and has a strong astringency, and a remarkable roughness on the tongue; but when it is ripe, has an uncommon sweetness, and a strong, unpleasant smell, like that of bugs. This tree grows in very great plenty, and is a kind of sweet acacia, being like to the acacia arabica. The inhabitants make a considerable harvest of the fruit, which is a great part of their sustenance. They reduce it to flour, and sometimes mix it with that of Indian wheat: when diluted with cold water, they call it anapa. The flour alone, which is very gummy, and sticks together, they press into cakes, or square boxes, and preserve it for food: this they call patay. Of the pods bruised they make a very strong drink, or chica, by letting it stand, from twelve to twenty-four hours, infused in a sufficient quantity of cold water; in which time it ferments, becomes very strong and heady, and occasions heavy drunkenness. A great quantity of proof spirit might be drawn from this chica; but the inhabitants are not sufficiently skilful for that purpose. More to the southward, this tree does not grow so large, and in the country of the Tehuelhets, it dwindles to a small shrub, not more than a yard in height. I have seen the fruit of this tree given, in consumptions arising from profuse sweats, and hectics, either in patay or chica, with great success; nor are those disorders common among the people who use it for food.

There is another species of this kind of tree, which I take to be the true acacia of the Arabs. It's leaves are like those of the algarrova, but the flower and fruit are very different. The flowers are of a fine yellow colour, very small,

(32)

fmall, grow together in a round heap, and have a very aromatic fmell. The pods are thicker, very black, with feeds like lentils, but harder. They have a gummy quality, a ftrong, aftringent tafte, and, with copperas, make a black ink, dying cloth and linen black; for which purpofe they are ufed by the inhabitants. The wood is more firm, and it's colour is of a deeper red, than that of the algarrova, and it weeps a gum, exactly the fame as the common gum arabic.

There is a third fort, that is not fo lofty, whofe pod is of a dull red, inclining fomewhat to brown; it is neither aftringent nor fweet; but the natives make a chicha of it, with which they cure themfelves of the *lues venerea*. It's operation is fudorific, and I have fometimes known cures performed by it, which in England would have required a falivation.

I have alfo feen a fourth kind of thefe pods, which came from the Chaco, and were much larger and ftronger, and their colour was of a deeper red, than any of the former. They were very aftringent and balfamic, had a ftrong fmell, like cyprefs wood, and were the fruit (as the miffionary who brought them affured me) of a large, thorny tree, without leaves. I believe that they are balfamic, aftringent vulneraries, and might be of great ufe in phyfic, at leaft in outward applications.

The miftol is, in this country, a low, knotty, crooked tree; in hotter countries it grows taller and more ftraight; and in the colder parts, to the fouth of St. Jago, it does not grow at all. The Indians ufe it for their lances, it being a very heavy and tough wood. It bears a fruit of a red colour, as big as a chefnut; the cortical part of which is very thin, and it contains a large, hard ftone. The natives eat the
rind,

(33)

rind, and the small quantity of flesh that is under it, and likewise make a chica of it, which is very sweet.

The channar, in the warmer climates, is a thick, tall tree, though not so large as here, more to the south. It's branches are very crooked and thorny. It's trunk is always green, and has a thin bark, like parchment, that dries, peels off, and is succeeded by a new one. It makes good fire and charcoal. It's wood is hard and firm, inclining to a yellow colour. The Indians use it chiefly for stirrups, though it seems capable of other uses, such as building, &c. It's leaves are small and oval; it's fruit is like that of the miftol, though less; neither is it so sweet, or of so red a colour. It's uses are the same as those of the miftol.

The molie is a great tree, not to be found to the south of the Province of Tucuman. The timber of this tree is of a very fine grain, and extremely beautiful; but of little use, on account of it's being so very subject to be worm-eaten. There are two forts of it; one, which has a leaf of the bignefs of a bay leaf, and bearing a resemblance to it; the other is exactly the same, only smaller. They are both evergreens, and their leaves, when bruised, serve to tan the fine goatskin leather, made in this country. Their trunks weep a considerable quantity of gum, which is used as incense, being very odoriferous. That with the larger leaves bears great plenty of a black fruit, which, when ripe, has a skin of a very light blue colour, almost white. It is about the size of a currant, and many of them grow in a clufter, like cherries. They are even sweeter than the algarrova; and, being boiled in water, they produce an extract or syrup, very sweet, and hot in the mouth; being steeped in water, they make a chicha, much stronger than that of the algarrova, both in tafte and smell. The drunken-

K   nefs

(34)

neſs it occaſions generally laſts two or three days, and gives a wild, glaring appearance, to the eyes of thoſe who are intoxicated with it: a certain proof of the ſtrength and quantity of the ſpirit it contains.

There are many other very beautiful and uſeful trees, and of a vaſt height, that grow chiefly in the deep vales, and breaks of the high mountains: among which are the white and red quiabrahacho, the viraro, the lapacho, the cedar, the timbo, the wild walnut-tree; together with the laurel and the willow. Theſe laſt grow there very tall and thick, but are not of much uſe.

The white and red quiabrahacho (or break-axe) ſo called from their extreme hardneſs, grow in the woods, in the plain countries northward of Cordova. In St. Jago they grow to the height of eight or ten yards, very ſtraight, and proportionably thick. The former of theſe trees has leaves reſembling thoſe of our box, but ſomething larger, with a ſharp, thorny point: the wood being alſo like boxwood, but of a red colour at the heart. It is very good timber, of a fine grain, but very brittle, hard to work, and exceedingly heavy. The latter is a different kind of tree. It's leaves grow in the manner of thoſe of the yew tree; it is more lofty and heavier than the white quiabrahacho; and it's timber is as red as blood, and can only be worked while it is green; for after it has been kept ſome time, it becomes ſo very hard, that no tool can touch it. In hardneſs and colour it bears ſo ſtrong a reſemblance to red marble, that it is a difficult matter to diſtinguiſh them.

The viraro affords a wood of a white colour, like our elm, and is uſed for beams, or any other ſuch purpoſes. It is very durable, and is eaſy to be worked.

The

(35)

The lapacho is one of the moſt valuable timber trees of theſe countries. I never ſaw it growing, but have often ſeen large beams, &c. of it, of eight or nine yards in length, which were to be ſent into Spain, for the uſe of their oil-mills, to cruſh the olives. The timber is of a duſky, green colour, has a good grain, and is not ſo brittle as the quiabrahacho, but is very hard and heavy.

The cedars are like ours. The timbo is a kind of coarſe cedar, which grows on the banks of rivers.

The wild walnut-trees are very large and lofty. I have ſeen ſome that were brought, worked and ſquared, from Tucuman, which meaſured twelve yards in length. They bear no fruit, and their leaf is like that of our walnut-tree, but ſomething bigger. In ſome of the deep vallies among the mountains, I have ſeen cedars and wild walnut-trees, that I judged might meaſure from fifteen to twenty yards in height, as ſtraight as an arrow. All theſe grow wild; with many other excellent timber trees, almoſt all of which bear thorns. Among which it may not be improper to mention the lanza; ſo called, becauſe of this the natives make ſpears and lances. This tree is of a yellow colour, very ſtraight, is excellent timber, and makes the beſt axle-trees for carts and coaches.

The inhabitants cultivate many fruit trees which grow wild in Paraguay, as lemons, and oranges both ſweet and ſour. Peaches, both cultivated and wild, are in great abundance. In Cordova and Mendoza, they have apples and pears of many kinds, pomegranates, apricots, plums, and cherries. In ſome places, figs almoſt grow wild, or at leaſt with very little culture; and alſo the Indian fig. This country, in ſome parts of it, produces vines; which in Mendoza, Rioia, and San Juan, are very much cultivated;

as

(36)

as also in the vale of Catamarca, and at Cordova, where there are some few vineyards. The wine which is produced is partly for private use, and partly to sell at Buenos-Ayres, Tucuman, Salta, Injuy, &c. This commodity is sometimes very cheap, and would be much more so, was it not for the heavy taxes it pays, in the cities to which it is sent.

Corn, and almost all manner of grain, is cultivated, and flourishes, in the jurisdictions of Cordova, St. Jago, and Rioia, when it can be watered ; and likewise in Buenos-Ayres and Santa Fe, if the year is not too dry. This article might be in great plenty ; and very great quantities might be produced more to the south ; but the Indians do not sow. The Moluches alone clean the earth a little, without ploughing, and set as much as they are able to cut with their knives. In Tucuman, the country is too moist for corn ; but the inhabitants gather great crops of maize, or Indian wheat, which they exchange for corn with those of St. Jago.

One of the chief articles of commerce at St. Jago is wax and honey ; which are found, in great plenty, in the vast woods on the other side of the river Salado. Great quantities of these commodities are taken from the hollow parts of decayed trees, and sold all over the neighbouring provinces. There is likewise a kind of honey, called alpamisqua, made by a very small bee. It is worked in holes under ground, in stony countries ; it's taste is a four sweet ; it is very diuretic, and extremely good for the stone and gravel.

Another, and a very considerable product of this country (though as yet unnoticed) is salt petre ; which might be gathered in vast quantities, if diligently attended to ; as there is an immense tract of salt territory, of about two hundred

or

(37)

or two hundred and fifty leagues in length, and from forty
to fifty leagues wide. It begins at about twelve leagues to
the north of the mountains of the Vuulcan, and extends
itfelf in breadth to Cape St. Anthony. It takes in all the
jurifdiction of Buenos-Ayres, and the fouth and weft fide of
the river of Plata, and, leaving Cordova to the weft, runs
through all the territory of Santa Fe, as far as the city of
the Corientes, at the junction of the famous rivers of Paraguay and Parana. It's breadth is here fo very extenfive, as
to comprehend all that part of the diftrict of St. Jago, which
lies to the weft of the river Dulce, and all the plain country
of Rioia, as far as the limits of the vale of Catamarca. This
is evident, from the brackifh tafte of all the brooks and
rivers which pafs through this falt foil; whofe waters are
not fit to be drunk, till they enter the Parana. All the
fprings in this great tract of country are more or lefs falt.
But the rivers which flow from the mountains of Cordova,
Tucuman, Choromoros, and Anconquixa, are excellent
water where they firft break forth, and continue fo for
many leagues; when they either reach the Parana, or are
fwallowed up in the falt lakes. A confiderable quantity of
falt is made of the earth, for private ufe, in the city of
the Affumption, in Paraguay; but it appears in the greateft
plenty in the neighbourhood of the Rioia and St. Jago.
After a fhower of rain, the earth becomes white with the
faltpetre, and is extremely chilling to the feet. It may
then, with a brufh or a feather, be gathered in great abundance, with very little earth; as likewife by taking the rain
water from the lakes. The people of thefe parts gather
little more than what they ufe for the making of gunpowder;
which is prepared chiefly for their feafts. I have frequently
bought fmall quantities of it, of about twenty pounds

L   weight,

(38)

weight, coarfely purified from the filth; all in fmall cryftal cylinders, without any cubes; which proves that it is unmixed with fal gem; which our faltpetre is not fo free from. This difcovery might be attended with great advantages, if proper attention was paid to it; as the faltpetre might be carried in boats, by the river Salado, to Santa Fe, and from thence, by the Parana, to Buenos-Ayres.

The greateft commerce of this country is that of cattle. There are every where very numerous flocks of fheep; and, at my firft going thither, the horned cattle were fo abundant, that (befides the herds of tame cattle) they ran, in vaft droves, wild and without owners, in the plains on both fides of the rivers Parana, Uruguay, and the river of Plata; and covered all the plains of Buenos-Ayres, Mendoza, Santa Fe, and Cordova. But the covetoufnefs and neglect of the Spaniards have deftroyed fuch vaft numbers of the wild cattle, that, had it not been for the providential care of fome few particular people, flefh would, at this time, have been extremely dear in thofe parts. On my firft arrival in this country, not a year paffed, but from five to eight fhips fet fail from Buenos-Ayres, laden chiefly with hides. Immenfe flaughters were made, without more gain than the fat, fuet, and hides; the flefh being left to rot. The annual confumption of cattle, flain in this manner alone, in the jurifdiction of this one city and Santa Fe, did not amount to lefs than fome hundreds of thoufands. Nor is the practice entirely laid afide at this time. Yet, notwithstanding, cattle are cheap; and, even in Cordova, bullocks are fold for two dollars a head; but formerly they would not have been eftimated at more than half the prefent price.

There

(39)

There is likewife great plenty of tame horfes, and a prodigious number of wild ones. The price of a two or three
year old colt is half a dollar, or about two fhillings and
fourpence; of a horfe fit for fervice, two dollars; and of
a mare, three rials, and fometimes only two. The wild
horfes have no owners, but wander, in great troops, about
thofe vaft plains, which are terminated, to the eaftward, by
the province of Buenos-Ayres and the ocean, as far as the
mouth of the Red River; to the weftward, by the mountains
of Chili and the firft Defaguadero; to the north, by the
mountains of Cordova, Yacanto, and Rioia; and to the
fouth, by the woods which are the boundaries of the
Tehuelhets and Diuihets. They go from place to place,
againft the current of the winds; and, in an inland expedition which I made in 1744, being in thefe plains for the
fpace of three weeks, they were in fuch vaft numbers, that,
during a fortnight, they continually furrounded me. Sometimes they paffed by me, in thick troops, on full fpeed, for
two or three hours together; during which time, it was with
great difficulty that I and the four Indians, who accom-
panied me on this occafion, preferved ourfelves from being
run over and trampled to pieces by them. At other times,
I have paffed over this fame country, and have not feen
any of them.

This great plenty of horfes and horned cattle is fuppofed
to be the reafon, why the Spaniards and the Indians do not
cultivate their lands with that care and induftry which they
require, and that idlenefs prevails fo much among them.
Any one can with eafe have, or train up, a troop of horfes;
and being accoutred with his knife and lazo, or fnare of
hiderope, he has wherewith to get his livelihood; cows
and calves being in great abundance, and out of their owners
fight;

fight; fo that it is an eafy matter to kill them, without being difcovered : which practice is very much followed.

There have been various attempts towards the difcovery of mines in this country; but they have all proved abortive. Some traces of a gold mine were difcovered, in the jurifdiction of Cordova, in the vale of Punillia; but, after much labour and expenfe, the quantity of gold was very inconfiderable, and the undertakers were ruined. The fame fate attended the workers of another gold mine, found near the mouth of the Plata, in the mountains near Maldonado; which was abandoned from the fame motives as the former. About ten years ago, there was a great noife about filver mines near the mountain of Anconquixa, and at firft fome quantity of filver was obtained. With this encouragement, the governor of the province interefted himfelf in it, notice was given of it to the King of Spain, and many expended their fortunes in the undertaking; but, after two years failure, it was given up, like the two former.

A few years ago, there was another difcovery made of fome filver mines, near Mendoza, at the foot of the Cordillera; which, after fome trials, yielded a large quantity of ore. The undertakers were at a very great expenfe, in procuring engines, and all the other apparatus neceffary to carry on the work; but, before I left the country, fome very unfavourable accounts had been received concerning thefe mines: fo that I cannot pretend to determine whether they have fucceeded or not. Even the famous filver mines of Potofi are very confiderably diminifhed. The quantity of ore taken from thence is decreafed near two thirds, and the Indians who ufed to work them are almoft all of them deftroyed, for want of a good police; and befides, many

of

(41)

of the mines are overflowed, and are thereby rendered ufe-lefs and unprofitable.

There is a great probability, that there might be found as many gold and filver mines, in the country of the Indian Moluches, on the eaft fide of the Cordillera, as have been to the weft; but the Indians pay no attention to fuch difco-veries, and the Spaniards are afraid to pafs thefe mountains, to make any trial, left they fhould be attacked by the Indians.

There are likewife, in thefe parts, various drugs; which might be very profitable, if the inhabitants thought proper to attend to them.

In the jurifdiction of Tucuman, and the city of the Seven Currents, there are great quantities of guaiacum, or holy wood, and of dragon's blood; which laft is a very valuable commodity. It flows from the tree upon incifion, and refembles, upon infpiffation, real blood; as well in colour, as in confiftence. It hardens, with boiling, or af-ter long keeping, to a kind of rofin; and becomes of a liver-colour, much darker than our officinal dragon's blood. It is likewife much more aftringent.

The balfam of caaci flows from a tree upon incifion, and is fometimes got by boiling it's boughs, very much bruifed. It is a hard gum, of the turpentine kind, but of a white colour, when got by boiling; otherwife, it is yellow and clear. It is a moft excellent incarnating medicine for wounds, and a fine vulnerary taken internally.

Two Indians were feverally wounded by a narrow lance, in the epigaftric region, juft beneath the xiphoide cartilage. The points of the weapons came out on one fide of the back-bone; a fmall degree higher in the one cafe than the other. What they drank iffued immediately out of the wounds.

M   They

(42)

They fuffered great pain, and had frequent lypothymies (or faintings) and cold, clammy fweats. I was ufed to apply this balfam externally, mixed with deer's fuet and marrow; but in thefe cafes, the wounds were clofed. I gave it them internally; and they took a fmall quantity of it, about the bignefs of a hazel nut, three times a day, and fometimes oftener in a lefs quantity. I had no other medicine in thofe defarts to give them, that could be of any fervice in their cafe. However, they were both reftored to a perfect ftate of health and ftrength; the one, in fix weeks, the other, in about three months.

I mention thefe two cafes as very particular ones, the ftomach having been pierced before and behind; a cafe generally efteemed mortal by the faculty. The narrownefs of the perforations (made by the narrow blade of a tuck, or fmall fword, converted into a lance) was, I imagine, the reafon of thefe cures being fo foon completed.

The balfam, or rather extract, called aquaaribaigh, is got by boiling a plant, which is a kind of fhrub lentifcus. In external applications, it is a good cleanfer and digeftive, and likewife breeds a good cicatrix. It is very efficacious, internally, in hemorrhages, dyfenteries, and catarrhs; being an agglutinant, and an aftringent, as well as a balfamic.

The gum ifica flows from a tree, and is gathered in Paraguay. It is called likewife trementine, that is, turpentine; but it feems to be a fpecies of gum elemi, though much hotter; and, when applied alone, it will raife blifters. It's chief ufe, in this country, is to make plafters for the fciatica; which it frequently cures. When tempered with an equal portion of wax or tallow, it makes a pretty good liniment of arceus; and is a good cephalic plafter, applied with oxycroceum, to the feet; which it never fails to keep warm.

(43)

warm. This is of great fervice to the Indians, and inhabitants in general; as they are very fubject to obftructions in
the liver, arifing from drinking too large quantities of cool-
ing liquors; and thefe diforders are attended with a great
coldnefs in the feet.

The contrayerva root is in great abundance. And in
fome parts of the mountains of Cordova and Yacanto, the
valerian and meum roots grow in great quantities, of a
much larger fize, and of a ftronger fmell, than any I have
feen in Europe. There are roots of the valerian as thick
as a man's arm. They have the fame kind of fmell as ours,
but, as I have juft before obferved, much ftronger. The
leaves of the meum are very large : It grows to a yard in
height. The flowers are white, and clufter together, in a
conic form, four or five inches high. It's ufe is well known,
in nervous diforders and epilepfies.

There are brought from the Guaranies two forts of roots,
of a plant, or flag, which the natives call fchynant; but,
though they bear the fame name, they differ very much
from each other. The one has all the appearance of the
common calamus aromaticus, though it is fomewhat ftronger,
both in tafte and fmell, and not fo large. The other has
very fmall, round roots, about half an inch in length;
very brittle, eafy to be pounded fine, and of the fame colour as the contrayerva. It has a very hot, fpicy, aromatic
tafte, and, when taken inwardly, is a very good medicine
in all cold affections of the brain and nerves.

Ginger likewife grows in thefe parts. But the commodity which might turn to the greateft advantage, if the
proper methods of preparing it were difcovered, is a
kind of tea, which I found about two years before my
departure from this place. It bears an exact refemblance
to

(44)

to the herb so called which comes from China; for, on putting some leaves of both sorts into boiling water, I could not discover, when they were displayed, any difference, either in their shape, or the disposition of their veins and fibrous parts. I found this tea plant, in very great quantities, in different vales; at the foot of the mountains of Cordova and Yacanto, near the mountains of Achala, and in the vallies of Calamochita; and, I have been informed, that, nearer Peru, in Tucuman, Salta, &c. it grows in greater plenty.

It is a shrub, from a yard to above two yards high. It's trunk seldom exceeds an inch in thickness, and is often less. It has no suckers near the root; but many long branches. It's leaves grow by three and three, in the manner of trefoil; they are of a beautiful green, and very smooth. It shoots out a long spike of blue flowers, something like lavender, but not so long, nor so well scented. To each of these flowers succeeds a small husk, each of which contains a seed, not bigger than a third part of a lentil, shaped like a kidneybean. After it is dry, on infusing it in water, it tinges the water in the same manner as green tea. It's taste and flavour are exactly the same, except that it is somewhat stronger, and is not so rough; but this difference is most probably owing to the freshness of it when gathered, or perhaps may arise from the different method of preparing it, or from not drying it on copper-plates, as is said to be done in China. In the drying, I could not make it become twisted and shrivelled, like the oriental tea.

I found likewise a lesser kind of this plant, both with respect to it's height, and the size of it's leaves.

There is yet another species of it, which grows in Chili. This has a round seed, without the husk; the flowers are
yellow,

(45)

yellow, and do not grow in a spike; and the leaf is not so smooth as that of the former, and is of a lighter green. On infusion, it gives a deeper tinge. The taste is much the same as that of the other sort, but not quite so pleasant, having a small degree of faintness in it's flavour. The Indian name is culem. The inhabitants of Cordova call theirs alvanhacca del campo, that is, wild basil; but this is a name given at random, to a plant, which bears no resemblance to the basil, either wild or cultivated; that being an herb, and not a tree.

As I and several of my acquaintance gathered some bags of this tea, and freely distributed it to many persons, I had an opportunity of trying it's effects; and found that it created a good appetite and digestion, cured many head-achs and inveterate apepsias (want of appetite), and anorexias (want of digestion), which had not yielded to any other remedies; in these particulars far excelling the tea of China. It is very remarkable, that, in the parts where this tea plant grows, there is the same kind of stone as that of which the China ware is made.

CHAPTER II.

A Description of the Indian Country, with it's Vales, Mountains, Rivers, &c.—Great River La Plata, with it's Branches, Fish, and Ports.

THAT part of the jurisdiction of Cordova, which lies to the south of the Rio Segundo, or Second River, was formerly the country of a great party of the northern Puelches, and reaches above fifty leagues, entering into the jurisdiction of Buenos-Ayres beyond Cruzalta. When I first went into those parts, I met some

(46)

troops of thefe Indians, ftill inhabiting the banks of the Second and Third Rivers; and there were fome few of them on the Fourth and Fifth Rivers. All the country which lies between the Second and Third Rivers is about twelve leagues over, and moftly woody; but, on approaching the Third River, the wood ceafes. The rivers that wafh this country all come from the high mountains of Yacanto, Champachin, and Achala; which are little inferior in height to the Andes of Chili, and are a kind of branches of thofe of Peru. All thefe rivers, except the Third River, after paffing through the breaks in the mountains of Cordova, and rufhing into the plains, in a few leagues lofe their fweetnefs, become falt, grow lefs and lefs by the drynefs of the fandy foil, and are finally fwallowed up in fome lake.

The Rio Tercero, or Third River, the moft confiderable of them all, before it paffes the mountains of Cordova (where it has a great fall) is increafed by the acceffion of the rivers Champachin, Gonfales, Del Medio, Quillimfa, Cachu-Corat, La Cruz, Luti, and Del Sauce; but coming to the plains, part of which are very fandy, during a dry feafon it difappears under the ground, and breaks out again at fome diftance. In times of rain it increafes very much, and brings down, in it's rapid current, great quantities of wood. It makes many windings, enclofing large fields. It's banks, for more than twenty leagues after it leaves the mountains, are full of high willow trees. The country through which it flows breeds excellent cattle, being fine pafture and corn land, and in fome places produces melilot, and a kind of woody farfaparilla. At the end of twenty leagues it grows falt, but is not fo very bad as to be unfit for drinking. In this manner it takes it's courfe to the Cruzalta, where it is called Carcaranna, from it's many windings,

and

(47)

and paſſes on, running from N. N. W. to S. S. E. till it enters the Parana, at the Rincon, or corner, of Gaboto, about eighteen leagues from Santa Fe.

There is nothing particular in the Rivers Quarto and Quinto; their produce is much the ſame as that of the former, except that there is a greater ſcarcity of wood in the countries through which they paſs. Their fields are ſtocked with cattle, and are fit for tillage. The River Quinto, when it overflows, has a communication by channels with the River Saladillo, which diſcharges itſelf into the River of Plata.

Between this country and the plains of St. Juan and Mendoza (the habitation of the ſecond diviſion of the northern Puelches, or Taluhets) are the mountains of Cordova and Yacanto. They form a continued chain, with very bad paſſes, through breaks of hills, and over aſcents and ridges, which are very ſteep, and unfit for wheel carriages. The tops of theſe ridges are from ſixteen to twenty leagues diſtant from each other. The intervening country contains many ſpacious and fruitful vallies, watered with brooks and rivulets, and beautified with hills and riſing grounds. Theſe vallies produce many kinds of fruit trees, as peaches, apples, cherries, and plums; and alſo corn, where the land is cultivated: but they are more particularly famous for breeding cattle, ſheep, and horſes, and eſpecially mules. The greateſt part of theſe laſt, which paſs yearly over to Peru, are bred in this country, and are it's greateſt riches, as they bring into it ſilver and gold, from the mines of Potoſi, Lipes, and all Peru.

On the weſtern ſkirts of the mountains of Yacanto, or Sacanto, there are many farms belonging to the Spaniards, who have been allured thither by the fertility of the ſoil,

which

(48)

which is capable of all kinds of husbandry, and is well watered by the rivulets which flow down from the mountains; and also by the facility of breeding cattle; there being few woods, except such as are necessary for fuel and building. And besides, the security from the annoyance of the Indians is another great inducement to settle there, as they infest those only, who live more to the south.

All the rest of the country to the westward, between these mountains and the first river Desaguadero, consists of plains, with little water but what the brooks afford. It contains abundance of fine pastures, but is unpeopled. Sometimes indeed the Taluhets and Picunches go thither, in small troops, to hunt wild mares, or rob passengers and waggons, which are passing from Buenos-Ayres to San Juan and Mendoza.

This country affords little for exportation to Europe, except bull and cow hides, and some tobacco, which grows very well in Paraguay; but it is of the greatest importance to the Spaniards, because all the mules, or the greatest part of them, which are used in Peru, come from Buenos-Ayres and Cordova, and some few from Mendoza; without which they would be totally disabled from carrying on any traffic, or having any communication with the neighbouring countries; as the high and rugged mountains of Peru are impassable but by mules, and in that country they cannot breed these animals. Those also which go thither are in general short-lived on account of their hard labour, the badness of the roads, and the want of pastures. So that the loss of this country might draw after it the loss of Peru and Chili. The road from Buenos-Ayres to Salta is fit for wheel carriages; but the mules, which are driven from that place and Cordova, are obliged, after so long a journey, to

rest

reſt a year in Salta, before they can paſs to Potoſi, Lipes, or Cuſco.

The people of theſe countries are very indifferent ſoldiers, and ſo diſpleaſed with the Spaniſh government, loſs of trade, the dearneſs of all European goods, and, above all, ſo many exorbitant taxes, &c. that they would be glad to be ſubjeſt to any other nation, who would deliver them from their preſent oppreſſion. Yet, notwithſtanding, all this country is without any other guard, than a few regular troops in Buenos-Ayres and Montevideo; and if theſe two places were once taken, the taking of the reſt might be accompliſhed by only marching over it; in which any enemy would be aſſiſted by the natives of the country. The loſs of theſe two places would deprive the Spaniards of the only ports they have in theſe ſeas, where their ſhips, which are to paſs Cape Horn to the South Seas, can receive any ſuccour. Before the expulſion of the Jeſuits from the miſſions of Paraguay, they might have had very conſiderable ſuccours from the Indian Guaranies, who were armed and diſciplined, and who helped to ſubjeſt the rebellious inſurgents of Paraguay, and to drive the Portugueſe out of the colony of Saint Sacrament, and were the greateſt defence of this important country.

That part of the Cordillera which lies weſt of Mendoza is of a vaſt height, and always covered with ſnow; from whence all this chain of mountains is called by the Indians Pſen Mahuiſau, or Snowy Mountain; or Liu, or Lio Mahuiſau, i. e. White Mountain. You paſs ſome leagues through very pleaſant vallies, encompaſſed with high hills, before you come to the greateſt ridge, which is very high and ſteep, with frequent frightful and deep precipices; and in ſome places the road is ſo very narrow and dangerous, on account

O of

(50)

of many huge, prominent rocks, that there is fcarce room
enough for a loaded mule to pafs along. The hollows are
never without fnow, even during the fummer, and in the
winter there is great danger of being frozen to death.
Many have loft their lives, by attempting to pafs them. before the fnows were in fome degree melted. At the bottom
of thefe precipices, there are many brooks and rivers,
which are as it were imprifoned, between hills perpendicular banks; and fo narrow is the fpace between them, in
fome places, that one might leap from one fide to the other;
but it is impoffible to defcend them. Thefe rivers and
brooks take many windings within the hills and precipices,
till they break out into the plains, where they compleat the
bulk of greater rivers. To afcend, and pafs over the great
ridge, is commonly one day's journey, at Mendoza and
Coquimbo, and much the fame in other places, according
to the information I have received.

Thefe hills produce very large and lofty pine trees.
Their growth is like thofe of Europe, but their wood is
more folid and harder than ours; it is very white, and
makes excellent mafts, as well as other materials for fhip
building, and is very durable; fo that, as Ovales remarks,
fhips built in the South Seas often laft forty years. The fruit
is bigger; the head that produces it being twice as large as
thofe which the Spanifh pines bear; and the pine-nuts are
as big as dates, with a very flender fhell. The fruit is long
and thick, with four blunt corners, as big as two almonds.
By boiling thefe fruits or kernels, they make provifion for
long journies, or to keep at home. Prepared in this manner, they have fomething of a mealinefs, and tafte very like
a boiled almond, but not fo oily. This tree produces a
confiderable quantity of turpentine, which forms itfelf into

a mafs,

(51)

a mafs, fomething harder and drier than our rofin, but much more clear and tranfparent, though not fo yellow. The Spaniards call, and ufe it as incenfe; but that is a miftake, as it has no other fragrance than that of rofin, only fomething finer.

The vales at the foot of the Cordillera are in fome places very fertile, watered with brooks or rivers, and, when cultivated, produce good corn, and a variety of fruits. Apple trees grow there wild, in great abundance; and the Indians make a kind of cyder, for prefent ufe, being ignorant how to preferve it.

The volcanoes, or fiery mountains, of which there are many on this fide of the Cordillera, may vie with Vefuvius, Mont-Gibello, or any of thofe which we know of in Europe, for their fize and furious eruptions. Being in the Vuulcan, below Cape St. Anthony, I was witnefs to a vaft cloud of afhes being carried by the winds, and darkening the whole fky. It fpread over great part of the jurifdiction of Buenos-Ayres, paffed the River of Plata, and fcattered it's contents on both fides of the river, in fo much that the grafs was covered with afhes. This was caufed by the eruption of a volcano near Mendoza; the winds carrying the light afhes to the incredible diftance of three hundred leagues or more.

The country of Buenos-Ayres, the antient habitation of the Chechehets, is fituated on the fouth fide of the River of Plata. The coaft here is wet and low, with many bogs and marfhes. The waterfide is covered with wood, which ferves for fuel. Thefe marfhes reach, from the banks, till you come to the rifing grounds; which are alfo in fome parts very boggy; being a clay, with very little depth of foil to cover it, till you go farther into the country; where

the

(52)

the foil is deeper. The country is every where flat, with fmall rifing grounds; and it is very furprifing, that in all this vaft jurifdiction, in that of Santa Fe, and of St. Jago del Eftero, there is not to be found one ftone, which is the natural produce of the country : and this is the cafe as far as the mountains of the Vuulcan, Tandit, and Cayru, to the fouth eaft of Buenos-Ayres.

The country which is between Buenos-Ayres, and the river Saladillo (the limit and boundary of the Spanifh government to the fouth of this province) is entirely a plain, without fo much as one tree or rifing ground, till you come to the banks of this river, which is about twenty-three leagues from the Spanifh fettlements. This country is near twenty leagues broad, from N. E. to S. W. and is bounded by the ftraggling villages of the Matanza and Magdalen. To the north of the Saladillo there are many great lakes, fome bogs, and hollow vales. The lakes I am acquainted with are thofe of the Reduction, Sauce, Vitel, Chafcamuz, Cerrillos, and Lobos. To the fouth eaft, there is a long and narrow lake of fweet water, near the river Borombon, which is very rare in this country; it is eight leagues diftant from the neareft Spanifh fettlement. About fix leagues farther is the great river, or rather lake of Borombon; which is formed by the overflowing of the lakes of the Reduction, Sauce, Vitel, and Chafcamuz, when they are fwelled with the great rains. It is fometimes near a mile in breadth, having neither banks nor falls, but a very broad, flat bottom. When it is moft increafed, it has not, in the middle, above a fathom of water. During the greateft part of the year it is entirely dry. After running about twelve leagues from the lake of Chafcamuz, it enters into the River of Plata, a little above the Stony Point, or Punta de Piedra.

From

(53)

From this river to the Saladillo is about twelve leagues, travelling S. E. The intervening country is low and flat, like the reft; and in fome places there is plenty of pafture, efpecially on approaching nearer to the banks of the Saladillo. In dry feafons, when grafs fails near the coaft of the River of Plata, all the cattle belonging to the Spanifh farms of Buenos-Ayres are driven down to the banks of the Saladillo, where the grafs lafts longer, by reafon of the greater depth of foil.

Thefe plains extend to the weft as far as the Defaguadero, or territory of Mendoza, and have no water, but what falls from the fky, and is gathered in lakes, except the three rivers of the Defaguadero, Hueyguey, and Saladillo. This country is not inhabited or cultivated, either by Indians or Spaniards; but abounds with cattle, wild horfes, deer, oftriches, armadilloes, partridges, wild geefe, ducks, and other game.

The River Saladillo, on account of it's faltnefs, is only drinkable by cattle. Almoft all the year it runs fo low, that at a place called the Callighon, eight leagues from it's mouth, where it is very broad, it fcarce reaches to the ankles; and, even at it's mouth, it would be impoffible for a fmall boat laden to enter: yet, about the beginning of October, I have feen it fwell fo prodigioufly, as to rife to the tops of it's banks in four and twenty hours, and to have, in the place juft mentioned, near a fathom of water, and to be almoft a quarter of a mile in breadth; all this happening, without any quantity of rain having fallen in that part of the country. The flood generally lafts two or three months, before it goes down. The Saladillo breaks out where the Fifth River (that paffes by St. Louis) ends in a lake; which, when it overflows with the rains, or melted fnows, that fall

P

from

(54)

from the mountains, caufes the flooding of this river. As it takes it's courfe by the diftrict of Buenos-Ayres, going afterwards to the fouth, approaching the firft ridge of mountains, then turning to the north, and again to the eaft, it receives the waters of many vaft lakes, that overflow with the heavy rains; and, when thefe fupplies fail, it almoft dries up. On the banks of this river, to about eight leagues from the mouth, there are many woods, of a tree there called tala, which is only fit for fuel or enclofures. The laft of thefe woods, called the Ifla Larga, reaches to about three leagues from it's entrance into the River of Plata.

The River of Plata is one of the largeft rivers in all America, and opens into the fea by a mouth near feventy miles broad. Some fay it is only fixty, and others extend it to eighty. It is called by this name from the place where it joins with the Uruguaigh: higher up the principal branch, it goes by the name of the Parana. Into which enter the great rivers Bermejo, the Pilcomayu, which paffes by Chuquifaca, and the Paraguay (from whence that province takes it's name) which paffes by the city of Paraguay or Affumption, and communicates, by navigable branches, with the Portuguefe gold mines of Cuyaba and Matagroffo, as alfo with Peru; in the fame manner as the Parana communicates with the mines of Brafil and the mountains of St. Paul.

On the banks of the River Carcarania, or Tercero, about three or four leagues before it enters into the Parana, are found great numbers of bones, of an extraordinary bignefs, which feem human. There are fome greater and fome lefs, as if they were of perfons of different ages. I have feen thigh-bones, ribs, breaft-bones, and pieces of fkulls. I
have

(55)

have alſo ſeen teeth, and particularly ſome grinders which were three inches in diameter at the baſe. Theſe bones (as I have been informed) are likewiſe found on the banks of the Rivers Parana and Paraguay, as likewiſe in Peru. The Indian Hiſtorian, Garcilaſſo de la Vega Inga, makes mention of theſe bones in Peru, and tells us that the Indians have a tradition, that giants formerly inhabited thoſe countries, and were deſtroyed by God for the crime of ſodomy.

I myſelf found the ſhell of an animal, compoſed of little hexagonal bones, each bone an inch in diameter at leaſt; and the ſhell was near three yards over. It ſeemed in all reſpeƈts, except it's ſize, to be the upper part of the ſhell of the armadillo; which, in theſe times, is not above a ſpan in breadth. Some of my companions found alſo, near the River Parana, an entire ſkeleton of a monſtrous alligator. I myſelf ſaw part of the vertebræ, each bone of which was near four inches thick, and about ſix inches broad. Upon an anatomical ſurvey of the bones, I was pretty well aſſured, that this extraordinary increaſe did not proceed from any acquiſition of foreign matter; as I found that the bony fibres were bigger, in proportion as the bones were larger. The baſes of the teeth were entire, though the roots were worn away, and exaƈtly reſembled in figure the baſis of a human tooth, and not of that of any other animal I ever ſaw. Theſe things are well known to all who live in theſe countries; otherwiſe, I ſhould not have dared to write them.

The River Parana has the extraordinary property of converting ſeveral ſubſtances into a very hard ſtone.

When it was firſt diſcovered, it was navigable, by ſmall ſhips, as high as the City of the Aſſumption; but, ſince that

time,

(56)

time, it has brought down so much sand, that even small merchant ships can go no higher than Buenos-Ayres. The larger veffels, and men of war, are obliged to unload at Montevideo. There is great need of good pilots for this river, to avoid foundering on the two banks, called the Englifh Bank and the Bank of Ortiz, or ftriking againft the Stony Point, which runs many leagues under the water, and croffes the whole river. The northern channel is narrower and deeper, the fouthern wider and more fhallow: oppofite to the bank of Ortiz it is not three fathom deep, with a hard ftony bottom. This river has two annual inundations, a greater and a lefs, proceeding from the rains, which fall in thofe vaft countries, from whence the Parana and Paraguay have their fources. The leffer is from the latter part of June to the latter part of July, is called the increafe of the Pequereyes, or Sparlings, and is ufed to cover all the iflands in the Parana. The greater begins in the month of December, and lafts all January, and fometimes February. This is fo high, that it rifes five or fix yards above the iflands, and fometimes more; fo that there appears nothing above the water but the tops of the high trees, with which the iflands of this river abound. In thefe feafons, the lions, tigers, ftags, and aquaraquazues, leave the iflands, and fwim over to the main land. On an extraordinary and uncommon flood of this river, the inhabitants of Santa Fe have more than once had thoughts of forfaking the city, for fear of a deluge; but when this vaft flood comes down into the River of Plata, it does but juft cover the low lands upon it's banks.

Some of the iflands of the Parana are two or three miles in length; they have great quantities of timber on them, and afford both food and fhelter to great numbers of lions,

tigers,

(57)

tigers, ftags, capivaras, or river-hogs, river-wolves (which I take to be of the fame kind as our otter in England) aquaraquazues, and many alligators. The aquaraquazu is a very large fox, with a very bufhy tail; aquara (in the Paraguay tongue) fignifying fox, and quazu, great. Their common little fox they call aquarachay.

This river abounds in fifh of many kinds, both with and without fcales; fome of which are known, and others unknown in Europe. Thofe that have fcales, are the dorado or gold fifh, the packu, corvino, falmon, pequarey, lifa, boga, favala, dentudo, and other leffer fry. Thofe that have no fcales, are the mungrullu, zurubi, pati, armado, raya or ray, erizo or water hedge-hog, many river tortoifes, bagres, &c.

The dorado is in great plenty in moft of the rivers of the Parana. They are very large, fome weighing twenty or five and twenty pounds each; their flefh white and folid; the head in general moft efteemed.

The packu is the beft and moft delicious fifh of any in thefe rivers, and has an excellent tafte and flavour. It is a thick, broad fifh, like our turbot, of a dark, dufky colour, with a mixture of yellow. It's breadth is two thirds of it's length. It's fcales are very fmall, and the head is fmall in proportion to the body. This fifh is in high eftimation, and is feldom found but in the fpring and fummer. When falted with care, it may be kept fome months dried, but after that time, being very fat, it grows rancid. I think it is fomething like our tench, though much larger.

Another fifh, in great efteem, is the corvino; which is only found near the mouth of the River of Plata, where the falt and frefh water mix together. They are as large as a middle-fized cod, and in fhape refemble our carp. They

Q

have

(58)

have very large, thick bones, and broad fcales. This fifh is very good, either frefh, or falted and dried. At the proper feafon, great quantities of them are taken with a hook, about Maldonado and Montevideo, and are fent to Buenos-Ayres, Cordova, &c.

The falmon is not at all like ours, and is a dry, unfavoury fifh, in no efteem.

The pequareys, or king's fifh (fo called by the Spaniards) are a kind of fmelt or fparling; in colour, fhape, and tafte, refembling ours, except that the head is very large, and the mouth very wide. Their fize is about that of a mackerel. They never frequent falt water; but are in great quantities in the River of Plata. When the Parana increafes, in the month of July, they go up that river, in vaft fhoals, a little above Santa Fe, to leave their fpawn in the leffer rivers, which enter the Parana. The fifhermen catch them with hooks, in great quantities, cut them open, and dry them, and fell them to the neighbouring cities. They are of an excellent tafte, and their flefh is very white, without any fat: when frefh, they are confidered as a great dainty. They muft be dried without falt, as it would immediately confume them; and if they get any wet or moifture, where they are hung out to dry, they will corrupt. They are in equal efteem with the packu and the corvino.

The lifa, in fhape, fize, and tafte, refembles our mackerel; but is not of fo beautiful a colour, nor fo fmall near the tail, and the fcales are larger. This fifh fwims no higher than the River of Plata; where the greateft fhoals are to be found near the mouth, in the high tides. With the full and new moon, they enter in fuch numbers into the little River Saladillo, that in one night, in two or three draughts

with

(59)

with a drag-net, I generally made a sufficient provision for myself and my companions during Lent.

The savala and boga are fish like our carp. In the Parana, and River of Plata, they weigh three or four pounds. All the rivers of these provinces produce great quantities of these fish, so that they are very cheap; and the inhabitants lay in a great stock of them, salted and dried. In eating of these fish, great caution is requisite, on account of the multiplicity and smallness of their bones. The boga, when fresh, is thought better than the savala, though that is both larger and broader. The method of taking them is with a net.

The dentudo (so called on account of it's large and sharp fore-teeth) is somewhat inferior to the last. It may weigh in general about a pound and a half, and, though well-tasted, is seldom eaten, as it has great numbers of very dangerous bones. It is the most thorny fish I have ever seen.

There is, besides these, a small, broad, flat fish, which is called palometa; it is thorny, but well-tasted. It has ugly, sharp fins, with which it wounds those, who too hastily lay hold of it. The wound which is made by these fins is very painful, shoots, festers, and inflames in such a manner, that it often brings on a fever, convulsions, and tetanus; so that it sometimes terminates in death.

FISH without SCALES.

The mungrullu is the largest fish found in this river. There are some that weigh a hundred weight, and are two yards in length. It has a smooth skin, of an ash colour, somewhat inclining to yellow, a bony head, rough gums, and a wide swallow. The flesh is of a pale red, and very solid.

(60)

folid. It is very ftrong and heavy in the water, and it requires very firm tackle, and great ftrength, to take it.

The zurubi is next in fize to the mungrullu, and not much inferior. It's head is almoft one third of it's whole bignefs, and is all bone. It has a very broad, flat mouth, and an exceeding wide throat. It's fkin is fmooth, of a white afh colour, fpotted like a tiger, with large, round, black fpots. It's flefh is white, found, folid, and well-tafted, and it is the beft of thefe fifh without fcales.

The pati, or patee, is not of a much lefs fize than the former, but has a fmaller head, and narrower fwallow, and has fome flefh upon the head. The colour of this fifh is like that of the mungrullu; it's flefh is of a yellowifh white; and it is efteemed almoft as much as the zurubi.

The armado is a thick, ftrong fifh, with a fhort body. It's back, fides, and fins, are all armed with ftrong, fharp points. When taken, it makes a grunting noife, and endeavours to wound; for which reafon it muft be ftunned, before it can be handled with fafety. This fifh generally weighs from about four to fix pounds; it's flefh is very white, firm, and folid.

The rayas, rays, or fkate, are fo very plentiful in the Parana, that the fhallow fandbanks are entirely covered with them. They are of an oval figure, near three quarters of a yard in length; the back is of a dark colour, and the belly white. They are flat, like ours, and have their mouth in the middle of the belly, which is indeed the greateft part of the fifh, the fkirts being very narrow, not above three inches broad, and much thinner than ours. As this is the only eatable part, they are in no efteem. This fifh has a long, narrow tail; at the root of which, on the back, it has a fharp, pointed bone, which has two
edges,

(61)

edges, rough like a faw with fmall teeth. With thefe, it wounds thofe who approach or tread upon it.

The wounds made by thefe bones are fometimes attended with very fatal confequences; for very frequently the bone is broken in the wound, and cannot be taken out, but by an incifion, very difficult to be performed in the tendinous parts of the feet. The wound becomes exceeding painful, inflames, does not fuppurate, brings on a fever with convulfions, which ends in an ophifthotonos, or tetanus, and caufes death.

The erizo, or water hedge-hog, is very like the armado, but not quite fo large. Befides being armed in the fame manner, it has a very rough fkin, full of fhort, fharp points. It's flefh is not fo well-tafted as that of the armado.

The vieja, or old woman, bears a refemblance, both to the armado, and the erizo. It is armed with prickles, but they are neither fo ftrong, nor fo numerous, as thofe of the abovementioned fifh. It's fkin, which is of a motley grey colour, appears to be full of wrinkles; it grunts like the armado, when it is taken; and it's flefh is very favoury. Thefe feldom weigh two pounds, and, in the fmall brooks and rivers, they are ftill lefs, not weighing more than half a pound.

The bagres are in all refpects, except their fize, like the pati: they very feldom weigh fo much as a pound and a half, and oftentimes much lefs. They have a ftrong, pointed bone, in each of the fins near the head, and muft be handled with caution after they are taken, as they live a long time out of water. Their flefh is foft and well-tafted. They are either caught in nets, or by angling.

I fhall here give an account of a ftrange, amphibious animal, which is an inhabitant of the River Parana; a defcription of which has never reached Europe; nor is there

R   even

(62)

even any mention made of it by thofe who have defcribed this country. What I here relate is from the concurrent affeverations of the Indians, and of many Spaniards who have been in various employments on this river. Befides, I myfelf, during my refidence on the banks of it, which was near four years, had once a tranfient view of one. So that there can be no doubt about the exiftence of fuch an animal.

In my firft voyage to cut timber, in the year 1752, up the Parana, being near the bank, the Indians fhouted yaquaru, and looking, I faw a great animal, at the time it plunged into the water from the bank; but the time was too fhort, to examine it with any degree of precifion.

It is called yaquaru, or yaquaruigh, which (in the language of that country) fignifies, the water tiger. It is defcribed by the Indians to be as big as an afs; of the figure of a large, over-grown river-wolf or otter; with fharp talons, and ftrong tufks; thick and fhort legs; long, fhaggy hair; with a long, tapering tail.

The Spaniards defcribe it fomewhat differently; as having a long head, a fharp nofe, like that of a wolf, and ftiff, erect ears. This difference of defcription may arife from it's being fo feldom feen, and, when feen, fo fuddenly difappearing; or perhaps there may be two fpecies of this animal. I look upon this laft account as the moft authentic, having received it from perfons of credit, who affured me they had feen this water tiger feveral times. It is always found near the river, lying on a bank; from whence, on hearing the leaft noife, it immediately plunges into the water.

It is very deftructive to the cattle which pafs the Parana; for great herds of them pafs every year; and it generally
happens

(63)

happens that this beaft feizes fome of them. When it has once laid hold of it's prey, it is feen no more; and the lungs and entrails foon appear floating upon the water.

It lives in the greateft depths, efpecially in the whirlpools made by the concurrence of two ftrcams, and fleeps in the deep caverns that are in the banks.

PORTS in the RIVER of PLATA.

The ports in this river, for fhips, are Buenos-Ayres, the Colony of the Sacrament, the Bay of Barragan, the Haven of Montevideo, and the Port of Maldonado. There are many others, for leffer veffels; chiefly at the mouths of the feveral rivers that run into it.

Buenos-Ayres (properly fpeaking) has no port, but only an open river, expofed to all the winds; and the more fo, becaufe the fhallownefs of the coaft obliges fhips to come to an anchor three leagues from the land. The winds here, efpecially thofe which come from the fouth, are very violent; and fhips are generally provided with cables and anchors of an uncommon ftrength, for this place.

The port of the Colony of the Sacrament is fomething better, by reafon of the covert it receives from the ifland of St. Gabriel and the higher land, and fhips being able to anchor near the fhore. Notwithftanding which, it is too open and expofed to the winds; and it has fome rocks and fhoals, and, in order to fteer into it with fafety, it is abfo-lutely neceffary to have a pilot.

The Bay of Barragan, which is twelve leagues to the fouth eaft of Buenos-Ayres, is likewife very wide and open, the land low all about it, nor can fhips of any burthen come within two or three leagues of the fhore. The only fhelter they have (if it may be fo called) are fome banks
under

under water, which break the force of the waves, but at the same time are very inconvenient, both for going in and coming out; and there is but little security, in a strong tempest, against a ship's breaking her cable, and being driven on them.

Montevideo is the best, and indeed the only good port, in this river. The Spaniards seem sensible of the importance of this place, by the extraordinary care they have taken to fortify it; having made it much stronger than Buenos-Ayres.

The entrance of this port is narrow, and through a strait made by two points of land. On that to the west rises a mountain, which may be seen at the distance of twelve, or even sixteen leagues; from whence this place derives its name. It is dangerous to sail too near the western point, as there are many rocks under water. The entrance to the east is deeper, and more safe. Beyond the western point there is a square battery, built close to the water. When I saw it, it was only of stone and clay, but since, I believe, it has been rebuilt with lime. The bay, from the entrance, is more than a league and a half in length, and the bay itself is almost round. Within it, on the east side, there is a small island abounding with rabbits, called in Spanish La Isla de los Conejos. The surrounding land is so very high, that no storm can reach this port (although there are very great ones in the river) the water being always as smooth as that of a pool; and there is sufficient depth for ships of the first rate. I saw one of that size here, which had formerly belonged to the States of Holland (and at that time belonged to the Marquis of Casa Madrid) that had entered to unload. The bottom is a soft clay.

Behind the battery is the small city of Montevideo, which occupies all that part of a promontory, that forms the

eastern

(65)

eaftern part of the bay. The fortifications are to the north.
Thefe are regular works, according to the modern rules of
military architecture; confifting of a line drawn from fea
to fea, or from the bottom of the haven to the river, enclofing all the promontory; of a bulwark, or angle, in the
middle, which faces the land-fide, and is well provided with
artillery; and of a pretty ftrong fort, with barracks for
foldiers, all bomb-proof. Towards the town, there is
only a wall, with a ditch on both fides of it. This place
has it's governor, and a garrifon of four or five hundred
regular troops.

The other fide of the bay is without any fortification, nor
has the high mountain even fo much as a watchtower; which
mountain, if occupied, might be a great annoyance to the
battery, city, and garrifon, on account of it's height, though
it is four or five miles from the latter.

The laft port is Maldonado. It is an open haven, at the
north entrance of the Plata, and is fheltered from the fouth
eaft winds by a fmall ifland, which bears the fame name.
Here the Spaniards have a fmall fort, where they keep a
detachment of foldiers. I know no more of this port,
having never feen it.

The northern fide of the River of Plata is an uneven
country, has very high hills, and fome ridges of mountains.
It is watered by a great many brooks and rivers; fome of
which laft are very large. The biggeft of thefe are the rivers
St. Lucie, the Uruguaigh, and the Rio Negro, which falls into
the Uruguaigh, about ten leagues from it's mouth. This
country is very fertile, produces all kinds of grain, when properly cultivated, and has alfo great quantities of good timber.
The rivers and brooks are all of frefh water. Here are a
great many farms belonging to the Spaniards; but the

S   country

(66)

country to the north of Montevideo is poffeffed by the infidel Minuanies.

The Charonas and Garoes (two of thefe nations) were formerly very numerous, but have been entirely deftroyed by the Spaniards. In this territory, there were formerly the greateft numbers both of wild and tame cattle; and here they increafe more than on the fouthern fide of the River of Plata. There are ftill great numbers of fheep and horned cattle, but few horfes. A great quantity of contrayerva grows in the neighbourhood of Montevideo; which is capable of all the products of Europe.

The Spanifh territory is bounded on the north by the Rio Grande, which divides it from the Portuguefe fettlements in the Brafils.

CHAPTER III.

Continuation of the Defcription of the Indian Country, with it's Vales, Mountains, Rivers, &c.—Terra del Fuego.—Falkland's Iflands.

TO the fouth of the town of the Conception (which is upon the fouth fide of the River of Plata) is the mount of the Vivoras, or Vipers; where are two thick woods, almoft round, with a fpace between them. About four leagues to the fouth of thefe is the Monte del Tordillo, or of the Grey Horfe, which confifts of a great number of woods, fome greater and fome lefs, each of them fituated on a rifing ground encompaffed with a vale; their trees the fame as thofe of the woods on the Saladillo.

(67)

Saladillo. All this is a plain, low country, with high watery grafs, and abounds in armadilloes, deer, oftriches, and wild horfes; and in the woods there are both lions and tigers. Some parts of thefe woods reach within two leagues of the feacoaft, which is extremely low, and fo boggy that it is impaffable, the boggy part being near a mile in breadth, and exceedingly deep.

All the way from the Saladillo to near the firft mountains there is neither brook nor river, nor any water but what is collected in the lakes in rainy feafons; and in times of drought even thefe fail.

About fifteen or twenty leagues to the E. S. E. or E. by S. of the woods of the Tordillo is the great promontory of Cape St. Anthony, which forms the fouthern point of the River of Plata. The figure of this cape is round, and not pointed, as is reprefented in fome maps. It ftands in a peninfula; the entrance into which on the weftern fide is over a wide boggy brook, or lake, which comes from the fea, or the falt water of the River of Plata. It is chiefly a clay, with fome little depth of foil, and is watered in winter by many fmall brooks, whofe waters have a falt tafte; but they are generally dry in fummer. The paftures are not fo good, nor the grafs fo high, as thofe of the Tordillo and the Saladillo. On the fouth fide of the promontory an arm of the weftern ocean enters, forms a bay, and terminates in lakes. Whether this bay might ferve as a harbour is not known, as it has never been founded; all fhips fteering very wide of the Cape, for fear of the great fand-banks called Arenas Gordas, or Thick Sands. I have been round fome part of thefe lakes, and paffed the channels by which others have a communication with the bay; but with great danger, not only from the bogs, but more efpecially from the tigers,

which

(68)

which were more numerous than I ever saw in any other place. Upon the borders of these lakes there are very thick woods of tala and elder trees, which are the retreats of these fierce animals, whose chief food is fish.

Towards the coast, there are three ridges of sand. That which is nearest the sea is very high and loose, and moves with the winds: at a distance it has the appearance of a mountain. The next is about half a mile distant from the former, and is not so high. The third is still at a greater distance, extremely low and narrow, the sand here being scarcely two feet high. The land between these ridges of sand is barren, being almost destitute of herbage of any kind. This peninsula abounds with wild horses, which (it is imagined) having got in from the neighbouring country, could not find their way out again; which circumstance occasions it to be a frequent resort of the Indian hunters. This small territory is called by the Spaniards the Rincon (or corner) of Tuyu, the country adjoining being called Tuyu, for more than forty leagues to the west. Tuyu in the Indian language signifies mire or clay, which is the soil of all that country, and continues southward to within ten leagues of the first mountains. The ridges of sand abovementioned reach south to within three leagues of Cape Lobos, having to the west of them low, boggy marshes, of two leagues or more in breadth, which extend all along the coast, before you come to the higher ground of the Tuyu, which begins at no great distance from the woods of the Tordillo. In this country there are a great many little hills, which run east and west, and about two or three leagues from each other. They are usually double; and at the foot of each of them is a lake, of one, two, and sometimes three miles in length : the most remarkable of which lakes are the Bravo, the
Palantalen,

(69)

Palantalen, Lobos, Cerrillos, &c. Thefe hills form in general high banks towards the lakes; which, without having any brook, river, or fpring to fupply them, feldom want water, except in times of great drought. They are called by the Spaniards Cerrillos (or little hills) and there are fome of them even on the other fide of the Saladillo.

This country, during fome parts of the year, fwarms with incredible numbers of wild horfes; and on this account the Tehuelhets, Chechehets, and fometimes all the tribes of the Puelches and Moluches affemble here, to get their flock of provifions. They difperfe their little moveable habitations upon the fmall hills beforementioned, and hunt every day till they have taken what is fufficient, and then return to their refpective countries.

Near the fea-fide, and almoft clofe to the great ridges of fand, is a great lake, called the Mar Chiquito, or Little Sea. It is about five leagues diftant from Cape Lobos, and is about the fame number of leagues in length, though not above two or three miles broad. It is falt, and communicates with the ocean by a river which paffes through the fand-banks. There are alfo three or four fmall rivers, that iffue from the north fide of the mountains of the Vuulcan and Tandil, and croffing the plain from weft to eaft, occafion fome bogs or marfhes, and empty themfelves into this lake. Thefe rivers are of fweet water, and have fome bagres in them, with great numbers of otters, as before defcribed: the largeft of them is that which comes from the Tandil, and enters into the northern point of the lake.

To the north of thefe rivers the foil grows confiderably better, the grafs being high and verdant, and fo continuing to the foot of the mountains; but there are no woods, nor

T   even

(70)

even fingle trees. The mountains, though they are not very high, may be diftinguifhed very plainly in a clear day at the diftance of twenty leagues, the country being fo extremely flat and level.

Thefe mountains are not one continued ridge, but many mountains or ridges of mountains, and between them are large, pleafant vales, which interrupt their continuation. They begin to rife at about fix leagues diftance from the fea-coaft, and continue for about forty leagues to the weft. They rife from the plain almoft perpendicular, and are covered with grafs till within about ten yards of the top; and from thence there are great numbers of ftones, which lie in fuch a manner as to form a wall, that enclofes the mountain, except at one end, where it declines gradually. The declining part is divided into hills and dales, with fmall rivulets, which join at the bottom, and form one common ftream. At the top there is a large country, with variety of rocks, hollows, and hills; with deep brooks, running among frequent breaks of the leffer hills: there are alfo fmall woods of a low, thorny tree, very fit for fuel. This variety of country is from two to three leagues in length, and fome-times a league in breadth, fometimes more, efpecially at that end where it declines. At the foot of thefe mountains there are abundance of fprings, which trickle down into the vallies and form brooks. The paths by which they are afeended are very few, and extremely narrow. Thefe the Indians ftop up, to fecure the wild horfes, &c. taken in the Tuyu, which they turn upon the top, as there is no getting from thence but by thefe narrow paffes, which are eafily ftopped.

Between thefe mountains there is a fpace, about two or three leagues broad, of a plain level country, with fome

few

(71)

few rifing grounds, watered with brooks; which fometimes run in the middle, and fometimes round them, and are formed by the fprings which iffue from the mountains. Thefe vallies are very fertile, have a deep, black foil, without any clay, and are always covered with fuch fine grafs, that the cattle which feed there grow fat in a very fhort time. They are in general very much enclofed by the mountains at one end, or by fome high hill which rifes in the middle; are moft commonly open to the north or north weft; and from the rifing ground there is a pleafant and delightful profpect a great way into the country, all the enclofed vales between the mountains being higher land than the plains to the north. I have not feen any country, in the diftrict of Buenos-Ayres, fo capable of improvement as this. The only inconvenience it is fubject to is the want of good timber for building houfes; which however, in the courfe of a few years, and with fome little trouble, might be remedied; efpecially as there are fufficient materials for temporary houfes, with roofs covered with reeds, which might ferve till better could be had.

The fmall rivulets, or brooks, that flow from the mountains, fometimes enter into, or form lakes; fome of which are more than a league in length. There is one of an oval figure, that reaches from mountain to mountain, and is in windy feafons very boifterous. There is alfo another, called the Lake of the Cabrillos, which is in the fhape of the figure 7, and is as long, but not fo broad as the former. On this lake there are great quantities of ducks, of various kinds and colours, fome of them as large as geefe; and on one point of it I faw fuch numbers, that it was a difficult matter to difcern the water, though wide. On one fide of this lake there are hills, and, on the other, a high, broken bank. At one

point

(72)

point there enters a small river, that comes from the mountains, and, having no immediate drain or channel to carry it off, breaks out, after running under ground, at the distance of a league, between the lake and the seacoast.

That part of the mountains which falls to the east, and is nearest to the sea, is called by the Spaniards Vulcan, from a mistake or corruption of the Indian name, Vuulcan, or Voolcan; there being a large opening to the south, and Vuulcan, in the Moluche tongue, signifying an opening. Volcanoes there are none; though the Spanish word seems to imply that there are such in this country. The middle part is called Tandil, or (as we pronounce it) Tandeel, from a mountain of that name, which is higher than the rest. The last point of this ridge of mountains towards the west is called the Cayru.

To the east of the Vuulcan, towards the sea, the country is unequal for about two leagues; after which it is flat, with brooks and watering places. Here are some thick and almost impenetrable woods, as well in the hilly as in the low country; in which are a great deal of the low, thorny tree, that grows on the mountains, and plenty of elder trees, which here grow very thick, and to the height of six or seven yards. The fruit is like ours, but very good to eat, being of a sour taste corrected with an agreeable sweetness. In other countries, to the north, as Buenos-Ayres, Cordova, &c. the fruit is of a bitter, nauseous taste, and the tree does not grow so high. Near the seacoast, about three miles distant from the sea, is a rising ground, which continues along the coast for about four leagues, and is exceedingly fertile, with rich pastures, where the cattle become extremely fat.

Near the shore, in this part, are two little, round hills, called the Cerros de los Lobos, or Hills of the Sea-Wolves.
The

(73)

The shore itself consists of high rocks and large stones. Here are great herds of sea-wolves and sea-lions (such as are described in Lord Anson's Voyage) who sleep on the rocks, and suckle their young in the great caves in them. In the woods there are many lions, but few tigers.

Lower towards the south, the coast for many leagues, as far as the mouth of the Red River, or the First Desaguadero, has perpendicular banks, of such a vast height, that it is frightful to approach the brink of them; but these terminate in low sands and sand-banks. All along this coast there are many small brooks and rivers, which, crossing the plains from the beforementioned mountains, enter into the ocean.

The country between the first mountains and the Casuhati is plain and open, and the Indians are commonly four days in passing it, when they travel without tents. The Chechehets, who travel to the Red River, go straight from the Vuulcan, nearer to the coast, and pass between the Casuhati and the sea, about fifteen leagues to the east of that mountain, and as much from the sea to the west; that they may avoid a vast, sandy desart, called Huecuvu Mapu, or the Devil's Country; where they and their families might be overwhelmed, if a wind should arise at the time they are passing over it.

The Casuhati is the beginning of a great chain of mountains, which forms a kind of triangle, whereof this makes one angle; and from hence one side of the triangle extends to the Cordillera of Chili, and another terminates in the Straits of Magellan; yet not without being sometimes interrupted by vallies, and continued chains of mountains, that run from north to south, with many windings. That part which forms the Casuhati is by much the highest. In the centre of some lower hills rises a very lofty mountain, that is as high as the Cordillera, and is always covered with snow;

U   and

(74)

and it is very feldom that any Indian ventures to the top of it. From this high mountain all this part derives it's name; Cafu in the Puel tongue, denoting hill or mountain, and Hati, or Hatee, high. The Moluches call it Vuta Calel, or Great Bulk. Some brooks and ftreams break out from the fouthern part of this mountain, that have deep banks covered with willows, which ferve for enclofures to fecure the cattle of the Indians. After running more to the fouth, they join and form a fmall river, which, running fouth eaft, enters into the Hueyque Leuvu, or Little River of Sauces, at fome diftance from it's mouth. The hills of the Cafuhati, after continuing about three or four leagues to the weft, have an opening of about three hundred yards wide, which they who take this rout (and not that between the Cafuhati and the Red River) are obliged to pafs. It is called the Guamini, or Guaminee, and has on both fides of it very fteep hills. All the country near thefe hills is open and pleafant, and abounding in paftures. The good enclofures that the hills and brooks afford for the cattle, and the plains to the weft-ward having plenty of game, occafion it to be conftantly in-habited by Indians of different nations; who fucceed each other according to their ftrength, the weakeft being always obliged to leave the place.

To the weftward of the vaft country of the Tuyu, down to the woods which are over againft the Cafuhati, is the coun-try of the Dihuihets; having thefe woods to the fouth, the Taluhets and jurifdiction of Cordova to the north, and the Pehuenches to the weft. That part of this country which falls to the eaftward is open and champaign, with very few woods or coppices, but is fubject to frequent inundations in fome parts, from the great fall of rains and the overflowing of many extenfive lakes. Some of thefe, which lie to the weft

(75)

weſt and the ſouth of this country, produce as fine a cryſtal-line-grained ſalt as thoſe of St. Lucar. The Spaniards of Buenos-Ayres take a journey every year to theſe lakes, with a guard of ſoldiers, to defend them and their cattle from the attacks of the Indians, and load two or three hundred carts with this neceſſary commodity. The diſtance from Buenos-Ayres to theſe ſalt lakes is about one hundred and fifty leagues. They are very large and broad, and ſome of them encompaſſed with wood to a conſiderable diſtance. Their banks are white with the ſalt; which needs no other prepa-ration, than being a little expoſed to the ſun and dried.

Farther to the weſtward there is a river with very high, ſteep banks; whence it is called by the Spaniards Rio de las Barancas, or River of Banks. It is called by the Indians Hueyque Leuvu, or River of Sauces, or Willows, which grow on it's banks. This river is of a conſiderable ſize, though little when compared with the Red River and the Black River. It is in general ſhallow, and may be waded, but has ſometimes great floods, from rains and melted ſnows. It is formed in the plain country between the moun-tains of Achala, Yacanto, and the Firſt Deſaguadero, or Red River, from a great number of brooks which iſſue from thoſe mountains, and takes it's courſe from thence ſouth and ſouth eaſt, till it paſſes within twelve or fourteen leagues to the eaſt of the Caſuhati, and enters into the ocean, after having received another ſmall river which flows from that mountain. But I have ſome doubts, from the relations of the Indians, that this river does not empty itſelf immediately into the ocean, but into the Red River, a little above it's mouth. All this country abounds with wild horſes, eſpecially the eaſtern part, that lies neareſt to the Tuyu and the mountains.

The country between the Hueyque Leuvu and the Red River

(76)

River is much the fame, but rather more abounding in lakes and marfhes intermixed with woods.

The Firft Defaguadero, or Red River, is one of the largeft that pafs through this country. It takes it's rife from a great number of ftreams that break forth from the weftern fide of the Cordillera, almoft as high as Chuapa, the moft northern town of Chili; and, taking an almoft direct courfe from north to fouth, abforbs all the rivers which flow from this fide of the Cordillera, befides a vaft quantity of melted fnow. It paffes, with a deep and rapid current, within about ten leagues of San Juan and Mendoza: near the latter of which places it receives the great river Tunuya, and another called the River of Portillio, that joins with it, and is foon after fwallowed up in the lakes of Guanacache. .

Thefe lakes are famous for the great numbers of trout caught in them, but more fo for burying as it were in their bofom fo vaft a river; becaufe here it feems to end, terminating in brooks and marfhes. But at a few leagues diftance it breaks out again, in a vaft number of rivulets, which, joining together, form one common river, called by the Picunches, Huaranca Leuvu, that is, a Thoufand Rivers; either from the many leffer rivers of which it is compofed, or it's great breadth; it being after this very broad and fhallow till it enters the ocean. The Pehuenches call this river Cum Leuvu, or Red River, it's banks being of a red colour.

In the winter, when the ground is hardened by the frofts, the Indians, &c. pafs over the marfhes without any inconvenience; but when, by the heat of the fun, the fnow melts in the Cordillera, the Defaguadero increafes to fuch a degree, that it overflows the lakes and marfhes, and renders them, as well as the Red River impaffable, except by thofe
who

(77)

who are dexterous fwimmers: an ability the Pehuenches and Picunches have not.

This river, from the part where the little rivers join it, directs it's courfe to the fouth eaft, till it approaches within a day's journey of the Second Defaguadero, or Black River; when it turns due eaft for about fifty leagues, approaching the Cafuhati: it then turns again to the fouth eaft; in which courfe it continues till it difcharges itfelf into the fea. The mouth of this river makes a large bay or opening, but is very fhallow, being ftopped up with mud and fand banks.

Sometime in this century a Spanifh veffel was loft at the mouth of this river, in the Bahia Anegada; the crew of which faved themfelves in one of the boats, and failing up the river, arrived at Mendoza. In the year 1734, or thereabouts, the mafts and part of the hulk remained, and were feen by the Spaniards, who at that time made an incurfion within land, with their field-marfhal Don Juan de Samartin, who told it me as an eye-witnefs. The courfe of this river therefore is eftablifhed paft all doubt.

The Tehuelhets of the Black River, and the Huilliches, in their journey to the Cafuhati, pafs this river in the two places where it takes thefe turns or windings to the eaft and fouth eaft. It may be near a hundred and fifty yards wide in thefe places, but not fo deep but that it may be waded, except when it is raifed by the rains and melted fnows. It is then fo deep, that the women and tents cannot pafs, and only the men who can fwim, with their horfes. The Chechehets, in their journey betwixt their own and the Spanifh territories, pafs it near the mouth.

The country which lies between this river and the River Sanquel (which difcharges itfelf into the Second Defaguadero) is full of marfhes, and woods of that thorny, thick,

X   rough

(78)

rough reed, that is called Sanquel in the idiom of the Pehuenches; so as to be impassable in any other manner, than
by going close to the Cordillera, and passing the river at it's
source, or where it issues from those mountains.

Twelve leagues to the west of the Casuhati, and about six
or eight from the Guamini, the Hueyque Leuvu before-
mentioned takes it's course. The way to this river consists of
hills, dales, stony mountains, and many woods. These
woods are so extremely thick, that they are passable only
through two strait paths, which lead to the River Colorado,
or Red River: one points to the west, and the other inclines
to the south. These woods continue above twenty leagues
to the north of the Colorado; to the south, they extend to
the Second Desaguadero, but there they are somewhat
thinner; and, to the west, they reach to the River Sanquel:
after which their thickness diminishes. At about five or six
leagues to the westward of the River Hueyque there is a
large salt pond, in the middle of the woods, and about five
or six leagues farther there is a second. There are likewise
two others; one to the south, and another to the north.
They are well stored with an excellent clean salt, of which
the Indians provide themselves great quantities in their
journeys.. There is also another very large salt pond not far
from the sea coast, between the First and Second Desaguadero.

From the River Hueyque to the First Desaguadero, or
Red River, is four, and sometimes five days journey, with
tents; which, at that part where it bends towards the south,
is through thick, low woods. From thence, travelling still
to the west, upon the bank of this river, with the woods to
the north, for five or six days more, you arrive at the place
where it comes from the north and doubles to the east; and
here

here it is paffed : when, after a long day's journey, directly to the fouth, over a craggy country encumbered with woods, where is no place to reft, the Black River, or Second Defaguadero, is feen from the hills, which are very high, running in a deep, broad vale, which is about two leagues in breadth on each fide of the river.

This river, the greateft of all Patagonia, empties itfelf into the weftern ocean, and is known by various names; as the Second Defaguadero, or Second Drain; the Defaguadero of Nahuelhuaupi, or Drain of Nahuelhuaupi; by the Spaniards called the Great River of Sauces, or Willows; by fome of the Indians, Cholehechel; by the Puelches, Leuvu Camo, or the River, by Antonomafia; and Cufu Leuvu, that is, Rio Negro, or Black River, by the Huilliches and Pehuenches. Where they crofs from the Firft to the Second Defaguadero, it is called Cholehechel.

The real fource of this river is not exactly known, but it is fuppofed to rife not far from the beginnings of the River Sanquel. It is formed by a great many brooks and fmall rivers, runs unfeen among high, broken rocks, and is ftraitened and locked up in a very narrow and deep channel; till at length it begins to fhow itfelf in a very wide, deep, and rapid ftream, fomewhat higher than Valdivia, but on the oppofite fide of the Cordillera. At a fmall diftance from it's firft appearance many rivers fall into it; fome of which are large, and come from the Cordillera, and enter principally on the north fide.

A Tehuel or Southern Cacique defcribed upon my table as many as fixteen, and told me their names, but not having writing materials at hand, I could not fet them down, and have fince forgotten them. He added likewife, that he knew no place in the river, even before the entry of thefe leffer

ones,

(80)

ones, that was not very wide and deep. He did not know where it began, but faid it came from the north. He was brother to the old Cacique Cacapol, appeared to be upwards of feventy years of age, and had lived all his time on the borders of this river.

Of thefe rivers which enter on the north fide, one is large, broad, and deep, and proceeds from a vaft lake, near twelve leagues in length, and almoft round, called Huechun Lavquen, or the Lake of the Boundary. This lake is about two days journey from Valdivia, and is formed by feveral brooks, fprings, and rivers, which come from the Cordillera.

Befides the river it fends forth to the eaft and fouth, which makes part of the great river, it may fend out another weftward, which may communicate with the South Sea near Valdivia: but this I cannot affirm, as I did not fufficiently examine it.

There is alfo from the north another fmall river, which comes higher up from the foot of the Cordillera, and croffes the country from N. W. to S. E. This falls into the Defaguadero about a day and a half's journey to the eaft of Huichin, the country of the Cacique Cangapol. It is called Pichee Picuntu Leuvu, that is, the Little Northern River; to diftinguifh it from the Sanquel, which alfo enters into the Second Defaguadero; each of them being called by the Indians the River of the North. The mouth of this river is diftant from that of the Sanquel about four or five days march.

The river Sanquel is one of the largeft in this country, and may pafs for another Defaguadero, or Drain, of the fnowy mountains of the Cordillera. It comes very far north, running between the mountains amongft deep breaks and precipices,

(81)

cipices, all the way augmented with new fupplies from the many brooks that join it. It's firft appearance is at a place called the Diamante, or Diamond; from whence it is called by the Spaniards Rio del Diamante. At a fmall diftance from it's fource confiderable brooks enter it, that come from the foot of the Cordillera farther north; and lower down, towards the fouth, the River Lolgen difcharges itfelf into it. This river is fo large, that the main ftream, by the Indians of the Black River, is indifferently called Sanquel Leuvu and Lolgen. It is broad and rapid even at it's firft appearance, and increafes by the many brooks and fprings it receives from the mountains, and from the very moift country through which it paffes for the fpace of three hundred miles, taking an almoft ftraight courfe from N. to S. by E. till it enters into the Second Defaguadero, or Black River, by a very wide and open mouth.

At the conflux of thefe two rivers there is a great whirl-pool; yet in this very place the Indians pafs it, fwimming over with their horfes. The current of the Sanquel throughout is very violent, efpecially on it's increafe. It's banks are co-vered with reeds and very lofty willows.

On the fouth fide of the Great or Second Defaguadero there enter but two rivers of any note. One is called the Lime Leuvu by the Indians, and by the Spaniards the Defaguadero, or Drain, of Nahuelhuaupi, or Nauwelwapi. The people of Chili give the fame name to all the great river; but this is through a miftake, they being ignorant of fome of it's branches; of which this is only one, and not fo big as the Sanquel, and much lefs than the main branch, even at it's firft appearance out of the Cordillera.

This river proceeds, with a great and rapid ftream, from the Lake of Nahuelhuaupi, almoft due north, through vales

Y   and

(82)

and marfhes, and continues it's courfe for about thirty leagues, receiving a great many brooks in it's paffage from the neighbouring hills, till it enters into the Second Defaguadero, fomething lower than that which comes from Huechun Lavquen, or the Lake of the Boundary. It is called by the Indians Lime Leuvu, becaufe the vales and marfhes through which it flows abound with ticks and blood-leeches, and thefe are called in the tongue of the Huilliches, lime, or leeme; and the country Leeme Mapu, the Country of Ticks; and the people Leeme Che, People of Ticks.

The Lake of Nahuelhuaupi is one of the greateft that is formed by the waters of the Cordillera, and (according to the account of the Chilenian Miffionaries) is near fifteen leagues in length. On one fide of it, near it's bank, is a fmall, low ifland, called Nahuelhuaupi, or the Ifland of Tigers; nahuel fignifying a tiger, and huaupi an ifland. It is fituated in a great plain, encompaffed by hills, rocks, and mountains; from which it receives many brooks and fprings, as well as water from the melted fnows. A fmall river enters it on the fouth fide, which comes from the country of Chonos, on the continent over againft Chiloe.

The other river which enters the Second Defaguadero from the fouth is but fmall, and is called by the Indians Machi Leuvu, or the River of Wizards; but wherefore, I know not. It comes from the country of the Huilliches, runs from fouth to north, and difcharges itfelf into the main river a little lower than the Lime Leuvu.

The Second Defaguadero from hence takes it's courfe to the eaft, making a fmall bend northward as it comes to the Cholehechel, where it approaches within ten or twelve leagues of the Firft Defaguadero; then it winds downward to the fouth eaft, till it enters into the ocean.

Some

(83)

Some fmall diftance below this laft winding it makes a large fweep, or circle, forming a peninfula; the neck of it is about three miles wide, and the peninfula, which is almoft round, is about fix leagues over. It is called the Enclofure of the Tehuelhets, or Tehuel-Malal. The river, till it comes to this enclofure, has high hills and mountains on both fides, but fo far diftant, as to leave, in many places, plains between them and the river of two or three miles broad, which abound with pafture for cattle, and are never fown: In other places the hills come clofe to the water. The banks are covered with willows, and it contains a few iflands difperfed here and there; among which there is one of a large fize, in the country of the Cacique Cacapol, where that chief and his vaffals fecure their horfes from being ftolen by the Pehuenches. I never heard of any falls in this river, or that it is fordable in any part of it. It is very rapid, and the floods are very extraordinary, when the rains and melted fnows come down the weft fide of the Cordillera, comprehending all that falls from thirty-five to forty-four degrees of fouthern latitude, being a chain of feven hundred and twenty miles of mountains. This rifing of the river is fo fudden, that though it may be heard at a great diftance, beating and roaring among the rocks, yet it hardly gives fufficient notice to the Indian women, to pull down their tents, and carry off their baggage; nor to the Indian men, to fecure their cattle by removing them to the mountains. Many difafters happen oftentimes in confequence of this great flood; the whole vale is deluged, and tents, cattle, and fometimes women and children, are carried down the vaft, impetuous torrent.

The mouth of this river, which opens into the Atlantic Ocean, has, I believe, never been properly furveyed. It is called the Bay Sans Fond, or Bottomlefs Bay; whether from

it's

(84)

it's depth, or it's fhallowneſs (as ſome imagine) I do not know, but I ſhould rather imagine from the former; for I cannot ſuppoſe that a river ſo extremely rapid, and which takes a courſe of near three hundred leagues, from the foot of the Cordillera, among rocks and ſtones, could carry along with it any great quantity of ſand; or, if it did, that the ſand could lodge at the mouth, againſt the force of ſo violent a current. The Spaniards call it the Bay of Saint Matthias, and place it in forty degrees forty-two minutes ſouth latitude; though in Mr. D'Anville's map it is placed two degrees farther from the line. I cannot think the diſtance is ſo great between the Firſt and Second Deſaguaderoes; all the Indians affirming that theſe two rivers enter into the ſea at no great diſtance from each other: wherefore, in my map, I have taken a middle diſtance.

In an expedition in the year 1746, to examine the ſeacoaſt, &c. between the River of Plata and the Straits of Magellan, the mouth of this river was not examined, although the captain of the ſhip was urged to make the proper diſpoſitions for ſuch an examination; but he neglected to give notice when he was got near to it's latitude. His reaſons for this conduct were, " that his orders were only to diſcover if " there was any port, fit to make a ſettlement, near or not " very far from the mouth of the Straits, that might afford " ſupplies for ſhips in their paſſage to the South Seas; that " he had ſurveyed all from Port Gallegos, without finding " one place fit for forming a ſettlement upon, on account of " the barrenneſs of the ſoil, and the want of the common " neceſſaries of wood and water; that he had done what was " ſufficient to quiet the King of Spain, with reſpect to any " jealouſies he might have of a certain northern nation's being " ſo fooliſh as to attempt a ſettlement in ſuch a country,
                                                              " where

(85)

" where as many as were left muft perifh; that the Bay Sans
" Fond was at too great a diftance from Cape Horn, to
" come within the circle of his inftructions; that his ftock
" of frefh water was fcarce fufficient to reach the River of
" Plata, and that he was not certain whether he fhould be
" able to get any more at the mouth of the River of Sauces."

A fettlement at the mouth of this river would be much
more convenient for fhips going to the South Seas than that
of Buenos-Ayres; where a fhip may be a fortnight, or a
month, before it can get out, on account of the contrary
winds, and then not being able to get over the flats but at
high water : and after this, it will take up a week, to get
down as low as the Bay Sans Fond ; when a veffel that failed
from hence might by that time have doubled Cape Horn,
and got into the South Sea.

If any nation fhould think proper to people this country,
it might be the caufe of perpetual alarm to the Spaniards; as
from hence fhips might be fent into the South Seas, and their
fea ports deftroyed, before fuch a fcheme or intention could
be known in Spain, or even in Buenos-Ayres. And farther,
a nearer way might be difcovered, by navigating the river
with barges near to Valdivia. Many troops of the Indians
of the river, the ftouteft of all thefe nations, would enlift
themfelves for the fake of plunder; fo that the important
garrifon of Valdivia might be eafily taken ; which would of
courfe draw after it the taking of Valparaifo, a much weaker
fortrefs; and the poffeffion of thefe two places would enfure
the conqueft of the fertile kingdom of Chili.

A fettlement is much more practicable here, than in the
Malouin Iflands, or the Ports of Defire and San Julian;
here being plenty of wood and water, and a good country,
fit for tillage, and able to maintain it's inhabitants. The con-

Z   veniences

veniences for a fettlement on the enclofure of the Tehuelhets are very great; it being defended by this great and rapid
river, which forms as it were a natural fofs, and containing
eighteen miles in length of a very fruitful country, abounding with paftures, and ftored with plenty of hares, rabbits,
wild fowl, deer, &c. and from the river it might be fupplied
with plenty of fifh of various kinds.

It is a confideration of fome weight, that the fettlers
might be provided with cattle, as cows, horfes, &c. on
the fpot, at a very trifling expenfe. A commerce might alfo
be eftablifhed with the Indians; who for fky-coloured glafs
beads, cafcabells of caft brafs, broad fwords, heads of lances,
and hatchets, would exchange cattle for the ufe of the colony, and fine furs to fend to Europe. And fo rare is it that
fhips meet in thefe feas, that all this might be done with fo
much fecrecy, that the place might be peopled and main-
tained many years, without the Spaniards being informed of
it. The French, for inftance, were fettled feveral years in
thofe fouthern iflands, without it's being known to the nations of Europe.

The woods hereabouts confift of the fame kind of trees
as are before defcribed, except one fort, which the Indians regard as facred, and never burn. It produces a gum, of the
confiftence; and almoft of the colour of yellow wax: on
burning, it has a very fragrant fmell, but is not like any of
the officinal gums ufed among us. I never faw this tree; but
the natives informed me it is but fmall. I have had fome
fmall quantities of the gum, which, mixed with wax, made
fmall candles.

All the feacoaft, from about twenty leagues to the fouth
of the Second Defaguadero, is a dry, barren country, with
very little pafture, and uninhabited by man or beaft, except
a few

(87)

a few guanacoes, that sometimes descend from the neighbouring mountains to the west. It has no water for a great part
of the year, and what it has is to be found only in the lakes
after great rains. At that season the Indians come down to
this country, to bury their dead, and visit the sepulchres,
and to seek for salt at St. Julian's Bay, or upon the seacoast.
Some few stony hills are dispersed here and there, and a me-
tallic ore, of a species of copper, was found in some of
them, at Port Desire.

In the voyage made in 1746, no river was discovered in all
this coast, though every where (especially in the ports described in the old maps) the Spaniards and missionaries
went ashore, and travelled all round the different ports.
This convinced them of the mistake they had been under;
which was probably occasioned by the strong eddies, or
running out of the water at the low tides. As for the River
Camarones, described in Mr. D'Anville's map, as opening at
the bottom of the Bay of St. George with three mouths (and
not in the Bay of Camarones, as I have seen it in former
maps) I have placed it in my map, upon his authority; but
at the same time must observe, that in the abovementioned
voyage no such river was discovered, though we entered into
this wide bay. The distance perhaps which the ship lay
from the shore might be too great for our making certain observations. The Indians indeed speak of a river in the
country of Chulilaw; but I could not discover whence it
came, or where it ended, or whether, being small, it was
not swallowed up in those deserts; as it often happens to other
greater rivers described in this map.

In the Bay of Lions the Spaniards went ashore, but did
not find any river. In the Bay of Camarones there was
nothing remarkable, but many huge rocks, that had the appearance

(88)

pearance of a city under water. The bottom of this bay was so shallow at low water, that the frigate was left upon the rocks, and was obliged to wait for the tide to get off. In the Gallegos Bay they likewise went ashore, but were called on board again, before a thorough inquiry could be made whether there was a river or not.

The territory of the Tehuelhet and other Patagonian nations borders upon the western parts of this uninhabitable country; and according to the relation of some Spanish captives, whom I rescued from slavery among the Indians (one of them had been seven years in that country) all this part consists of vales enclosed within low ridges of mountains, watered with springs and small brooks, which are swallowed up in little lakes, or watering places, that in summer dry up: so that many of the inhabitants, at that season, go to live on the Second Desaguadero, carrying their wives, families, and all their baggage along with them; and some go even as far as the Casuhati, the Vuulcan, and the Tandil.

These vales abound in pastures, and have some small woods, which serve for fuel. There are plenty of guanacoes in this country, and in some places they make their tents of the skins of this animal. There are likewise great numbers of antas, whose skins the Tehuelhets sell to the other Puelches, with which the latter make their armour.

The anta is of the stag kind, but without horns. It's body is as big as that of a large ass; it's head very long and tapering, ending in a small snout; it's body very strong, and broad at the shoulders and haunches; it's legs and shanks are long, and stronger than those of a stag; it's feet cloven like those of a stag, but something larger; it's tail short, like that of a deer. The strength of this animal is wonderful; it being able to drag a pair of horses after it, when one horse

is

(89)

is sufficient to take a cow or a bull. When he is pursued, he opens his way through the thickest woods and coppices, breaking down every thing that opposes him. I do not know whether there have ever been any attempts to tame this animal, though it is by no means fierce, and does no mischief but to the chacras, or plantations, and might be of great service, on account of it's strength, if it could be brought to labour.

There are no wild horses in this country, but the tame ones bred here are superior, both in beauty and strength, to any in South America; enduring long journeys, without any other provision than what they pick up by the way; and in courage and swiftness they are exceeded by none. There is also plenty of small game, and the Indians, who are very numerous, live chiefly upon it. There are likewise considerable quantities of the occidental bezoar, found not only in the stomach of the guanacoes and vicunias, but also of the anta; though in this last it is somewhat coarser. When it is given in a considerable quantity, it greatly promotes a diaphoresis. I have almost always found it give relief and immediate ease in heartburns, faintings, &c. the dose consisting of a dram, or two scruples, taken in any thing; though it might be given in a larger quantity with great safety. I have found it preferable, in many cases, to our testaceous powders, and mineral substances. I have had some of these stones that weighed eighteen ounces each.

There are many species of the fowl kind, such as doves, turtles, ducks, pheasants, partridges, &c. which I mention, as profitable, though not regarded or used by the Indians. There are also birds of prey, as eagles, vultures, kites, gleads, owls, and falcons. But, so far to the south, there are neither lions nor tigers, except in the Cordillera.

A a   The

(90)

The country of the Huilliches, over againſt the Tehuel Mapu, and to the ſouth of Valdivia, is, according to the relations of the miſſionaries, a very poor country, and deſtitute of all the common neceſſaries of life; as indeed is all that ſeacoaſt below Chili, to the Magellanic Straits. The people of the coaſt live chiefly upon fiſh, and are diſtinguiſhed by the names of Chonos, Poy-yus, and Key-yus. Of theſe two laſt nations, thoſe who live farther from the coaſt hunt on foot, being very nimble, and inured to this exerciſe from their infancy. In Chiloe, great part of the proviſions for the miſſionaries, and the garriſon of Spaniſh ſoldiers, is ſent from Valdivia, or other ſeaports of Chili.

In this iſland there is a ſmall city, or rather village, called Caſtro; where a Spaniſh captain, or deputy governor, reſides.

The mountains of the Huilliches are conſiderably lower than thoſe towards the north, ſo that they are in this country paſſable at all times of the year, and beſides have frequent openings. They are well covered with wood and even timber. There is a kind of tree peculiar to this country, which the Indians call lahual, and the Spaniards, alerce, or, according to our pronunciation, lawal and alerſey. It was not very particularly deſcribed to me; but I take it to be of the fir kind. What is very remarkable in it, is it's convenience for being ſplit into boards, it's trunk being naturally marked with ſtraight lines from top to bottom; ſo that, by cleaving it with wedges, it may be parted into very ſtraight boards, of any thickneſs, in a better and ſmoother manner than if they were ſawn. Theſe trees are very large, as I have been informed; but I cannot pretend to ſay what is their general diameter.

If plants or ſeeds of this tree were brought over into England,

England, it is very probable they would thrive here, the climate being as cold as in the countries where it grows; and it is there reckoned to be the moſt valuable timber they have, both for it's beauty and duration. It may not be improper to obſerve in this place, that by means of the rivers of Nahuelhuaupi, Sanquel, and Lolgen, great quantities of this wood, pine-trees, &c. might be ſent down, in large floats, to the Great River of Sauces, and ſo to the Bay of San Matthias, for the building of ſhips, houſes, &c.

The Huilliches have alſo a ſpecies of tobacco, which they bruiſe when almoſt green, and make into ſhort, thick, cylindrical rolls. It is of a dark-green colour, and when ſmoked yields a ſtrong, diſagreeable ſmell, ſomething different from the Virginia tobacco. It is very ſtrong, and ſoon intoxicates; ſo that they hand the pipe from one to another, and each takes a whiff in his turn, as the continuing it for any length of time would diſturb the ſenſes.

The country of thoſe Tehuelhets that live nearer and cloſe up to the Straits, as the Sehuau-cunnees, and Yacana-cunnees, is much the ſame as of the other Tehuelhets. They have within land ſome high woods, and a ſmall ſhrub, which produces a fruit very like our winberries, but ſomething hotter: they are good to eat, and very proper for the climate.

The Tierra del Fuego is compoſed of a great number of iſlands. Thoſe to the weſt are ſmall and low, full of marſhes and fens, and moſtly uninhabitable, being often covered with water; but thoſe which are to the eaſt are bigger, and higher land, with mountains and woods, and are inhabited by Indians of the Yacana-cunnees, and theſe have had frequent communication with the French and Spaniards, who went thither from the Malouin Iſlands to get wood. I cannot

(92)

not pretend to fay, whether in thefe large iflands there is any game, befides that of fowl: but it is highly credible, that the Indians who dwell there do not live entirely upon fifh, which it is very difficult to take during the winter in thefe cold climates.

In the year 1765 or 1766 (I do not remember which) a Spanifh fhip, laden with merchandize for Peru, was driven afhore and beat to pieces upon the Ifland del Fuego, about fourteen leagues (as they reckoned) from the Straits mouth. The crew being faved, they made themfelves a veffel, big enough to carry them and their provifions to Buenos-Ayres; where they informed the Governor, Don Pedro de Cevallos, that the Indians, natives of this ifland, were very humane and hofpitable, and helped them to carry down many very heavy trees, which they had fallen for the building of their veffel, and affifted them in every thing: that they had been very liberal of their cargo to the Indians, who efteemed thofe things leaft which were of the greateft value, as filk, fatin, tiffues, &c. and were more defirous of the coarfeft cloths, to keep them warm: that at firft they came down in great numbers with their arms, bows and arrows, and that their manner of expreffing a defire of friendfhip and peace was by laying down their arms, bowing their bodies, and then leaping up and rubbing their bellies, or beating on them with their hands. The Governor fent this account to the Court of Spain, and propofed the fixing a colony in this ifland; but the French being at that time tampering with the Spanifh Court about the purchafe of the Malouin Iflands, the prudent defigns of the Governor were fruftrated, and he was recalled to his own country.

Tamu, the Yacana-cunnee Cacique, told me that they ufed a kind of float, with which they fometimes paffed the Straits, and

(93)

and had communication with thofe of his nation: from whence it is evident, that this place has the conveniences of wood, water, and foil; and, if there could be found a tolerable harbour, it would be much more convenient for a colony, and have a better command of the paffage to the South Sea, than Falkland's Iflands.

The Malouin or Falkland's Iflands are many in number; fome are exceeding fmall; but there are two which are very large. What I fhall relate concerning them is according to the accounts which I have received from many of the Spanifh officers, who went to receive this country from the French, and to tranfport the Spaniards thither from Buenos-Ayres, as well as to carry away the French inhabitants; and alfo from a French gunner, who failed with me from the River of Plata to the Port of Cadiz, and had refided in thofe iflands feveral years. All thefe were unexceptionable witneffes.

Thefe iflands are fo low and boggy, that after a fhower of rain it is impoffible to ftir out, without finking up to the knees in mire. The houfes are built with earth, and from the exceeding moiftnefs of the country, are green within with mofs; and bricks cannot be made for want of fuel. The fettlers have fown various kinds of grain, as corn, barley, peafe, beans, &c. but the land is fo barren, that they all run into grafs and ftraw, and yield no crop. All the induftry of the French, for feveral years, could only accomplifh the raifing a fmall quantity of falad; and this they effected by gathering the dung of all their animals; cows, hogs, and horfes. The only animals which are natural to thefe iflands are penguins and buftards, and thefe laft are alone eatable. They are but indifferent food, are killed by fhooting, and foon grew fo fhy, that they became very dear. Some fifh are alfo taken, but in quantities by no means proportionable

B b

(94)

portionable to the wants of the inhabitants. So great is the poverty of the country, that the Spanifh Governor of Buenos-Ayres was obliged to be at the expenfe of fending fhips every three or four months, to maintain the people and garrifon, without any returns; and though live hogs, cows, and horfes, have been carried thither, yet the country is fo cold, fo moift, and fo barren of fhelter, that they never increafe; fo that thefe charges muft laft as long as the fettlement continues. There is no wood, and nothing that ferves for fuel but a low fhrub, fomething like our furze or heath, and this but in fmall quantities: the inhabitants therefore are obliged to fend fmall veffels to fetch wood from Tierra del Fuego. Water is almoft the only neceffary this country affords, befides the convenience of a good harbour; which yet does not appear to anfwer the end for which the fettlement was made: for as this Haven of Solidad lies open to the north or north eaft, a fhip muft have a wind from that quarter, to enter it. Now as fuch a wind is the moft favourable for paffing Cape Horn, a fhip would hardly enter here, and lofe the favourable gale that would carry her into the South Sea; efpecially as fhe muft wait for a contrary wind to get out again, and then for a north eafterly wind to fteer for Cape Horn; and all this in a place where there are no hopes of taking in any other provifion befides water. ...

The French fent people to thefe iflands in the time of the laft war, to fecure a port for their fhips coming from the Eaft Indies by the South Sea; which courfe they took at that time, to efcape the Englifh privateers: but when the war was over, being tired of fo wretched a colony, and fo many expenfes, which now ceafed to anfwer, they determined to leave them. But being defirous (if poffible) to recover the money laid out here, they reprefented their new acquifitions

in

(95)

in fo favourable a manner to the Spanifh Court, that the King of Spain agreed to pay five hundred thoufand dollars (fome fay eight hundred thoufand, and others enlarge the fum to a million) for their ceding them to Spain: whereof the King of France was to receive a part, and the reft to go to Monfieur Bougainville the proprietor; befides fome cargoes of goods, bought with this money in the Rio Janeiro, permitted to be fold in Buenos-Ayres. All this the captain of a Spanifh frigate reprefented, with a great deal of freedom, to the prefent Governor of Buenos-Ayres, in the prefence of Monfieur Bougainville; complaining of the trick put upon the King of Spain, and protefting that no perfon, commiffioned to receive thefe iflands, could, confiftently with the loyalty he owed his Sovereign, or his obligations as a Chriftian, upon feeing them, accept the delivery, till he had firft given an account of them to the Court of Spain; it being evident that they had been grofsly impofed upon. Monfieur Bougainville did not think proper to contradict what this officer had faid; who, befides being an unexceptionable eye-witnefs himfelf, could (if neceffary) have corroborated his account by the teftimonies of a hundred people, who were lately arrived with the exportation of the French inhabitants.

The Spaniards tranfported with their colony two Francifcan friars, and a governor or vice-governor; who, beholding their fettlement, were overwhelmed with grief; and the Governor, Colonel Catani, at the departure of the fhips for Buenos-Ayres, with tears in his eyes declared, that he thought thofe happy who got from fo miferable a country, and that he himfelf fhould be very glad if he was permitted to throw up his commiffion, and return to Buenos-Ayres, though in no higher ftation than that of a cabin-boy.

CHAPTER

CHAPTER IV.

An Account of the Inhabitants of the most Southern Part of AMERICA, *described in the Map.*

THE nations of Indians, which inhabit these parts, bear among themselves the general denominations of Moluches and Puelches.

The Moluches are known among the Spaniards by the names of Aucaes and Araucanos.

The former of these is a nick-name, and a word of reproach, meaning rebel, wild, savage, or banditti; the word aucani signifying to rebel, rise, or make a riot, and is applied both to men and beasts, as auca cahual is a wild horse, aucatun, or aucatuln, to make an uproar.

They call themselves Moluches, from the word molun, to wage war; and moluche signifies a warriour. They are dispersed over the country both on the east and west sides of the Cordillera of Chili, from the confines of Peru to the Straits of Magellan, and may be divided into the different nations of the Picunches, Pehuenches, and Huilliches.

The Picunches are the most northern of these people, and are so called from picun, which in their language signifies north, and che, men or people. They inhabit the mountains, from Coquimbo to somewhat lower than St. Jago of Chili. These are the most valiant and the biggest-bodied men of all the Moluches; especially those to the west of the
Cordillera:

(97)

Cordillera: among which are thofe of Penco, Tucapel, and Arauco; from which laft, the Spaniards by miftake gave the name of Araucanos to all the reft of the Indians of Chili. Thofe who live to the eaft of the Gordillera reach fomething lower than Mendoza, and are called by thofe on the other fide Puelches, puel fignifying eaft. But by others who live towards the fouth, they are called Picunches. I knew fome of their Caciques; whofe names were Tfeucan-antu, Pilque-pangi, Caru-pangi, and Caru-lonco.

The Pehuenches border on the Picunches to the north, and reach from over againft Valdivia to thirty five degrees of fouth latitude. They derive their name from the word pehuen, which fignifies pine-tree; becaufe their country abounds with thefe trees. As they live to the fouth of the Picunches, they are fometimes called by them Huilliches, or Southern People, but moft generally Pehuenches. Their Caciques were Colopichun, Amolepi, Nonque, Nicolafquen, Guenulep, Cufu-huanque, Col-nancon, Ayalep and Antu-cule. The laft was a young Cacique, whom I knew very well.

Thefe two nations were formerly very numerous, and were engaged in long and bloody wars with the Spaniards, whom they almoft drove out of Chili, deftroyed the cities of the Imperial, Oforno, and Villarica, and killed two of their prefidents, Valdivia, and Don Martin de Loyola; but they are now fo much diminifhed, as not to be able to mufter four thoufand men among them all. This has been in fome mea-fure owing to their frequent wars with the Spaniards of Chili, Mendoza, Cordova, and Buenos-Ayres, with their neigh-bours the Puelches, and with one another. But what has made the greateft havock amongft them, is the brandy which they buy of the Spaniards, and their pulcu, or chicha, which they make themfelves. They often pawn and fell

C c   their

(98)

their wives and children to the Spaniards for brandy, with which they get drunk, and then kill one another; and it feldom happens that the party who has fuffered moft on thefe occafions waits long for an opportunity of revenge. The fmall pox alfo, which was introduced into this country by the Europeans, caufes a more terrible deftruction among them than the plague, defolating whole towns by it's malignant effects. This diforder is much more fatal to thefe people, than to the Spaniards or Negroes, owing to their grofs habit of body, bad food, and want of covering, medicines, and neceffary care: for the neareft relations of thofe who fall fick fly from them, to avoid the diftemper, and leave them to perifh, perhaps in the middle of a defart. About forty five years ago, the numerous nation of the Chechehets, having caught this diforder in the neighbourhood of Buenos-Ayres, endeavoured to fly from it, by retiring into their own country, which was about two hundred leagues diftant, through vaft defarts. During this journey they daily left behind them their fick friends and relations, forfaken and alone, with no other affiftance than a hide reared up againft the wind, and a pitcher of water. Thus they have been brought fo low, that they have not more than three hundred men capable of bearing arms.

The Huilliches, or Southern Moluches, reach from Valdivia to the Straits of Magellan. They are divided into four diftinct tribes or nations. The firft of thefe reaches to the Sea of Chiloe, and beyond the Lake of Nahuelhuaupi, and fpeak the Chilenian tongue. The fecond nation are the Chonos, who live on and near the iflands of Chiloe. The third nation is called Poy-yus, or Peyes, and inhabits the feacoaft from forty eight to a little more than fifty one degrees of fouth latitude; and from thence to the Straits live the fourth
nation,

(99)

nation, called the Key-yus, or Keyes. Thefe laft three nations are known by the name of Vuta Huilliches, or Great Huilliches, becaufe they are bigger-bodied men than the firft, who are called Pichi Huilliches, or Little Huilliches. They feem likewife to be a different people; as the language they fpeak is a mixture of the Moluche and Tehuel languages. The other Huilliches, and the Pehuenches, fpeak in the fame manner with one another, and differ only from the Picunches in ufing the letter S inftead of R and D, not having thefe two letters in their alphabet: and the Picunches, having no S, ufe R and D inftead of it; and oftentimes T, where the others ufe CH; as domo, for fomo, a woman; huaranca, for huafanca, a thoufand; vuta, for vucha, great. Thefe nations are numerous, efpecially the Vuta Huilliches. The Caciques of the firft, or Pichi Huilliches, were Puelman, Painiacal, Tepuanca; whom I have feen; with many others, whofe names I have forgotten.

The Puelches, or Eaftern People (fo called by thofe of Chili becaufe they live to the eaft of them) are bounded on the weft by the Moluches, down to the Straits of Magellan; by which they are terminated on the fouth; on the north, by the Spaniards of Mendoza, San Juan, San Louis de la Punta, Cordova, and Buenos-Ayres; and to the eaft, by the ocean. They bear different denominations, according to the fituation of their refpective countries, or becaufe they were originally of different nations. Thofe towards the north are called Taluhets; to the weft and fouth of thefe are the Diuihets; to the fouth eaft, the Chechehets; and to the fouth of thefe laft is the country of the Tehuelhets, or, in their proper language, Tehuel-Kunny, i. e. Southern Men.

The Taluhets border to the weft on the Picunches, and dwell on the eaft fide of the Firft Defaguadero, as far as
the

(100)

the lakes of Guanacache, in the jurifdictions of St. Juan and St. Louis de la Punta, fcattered in fmall troops, and feldom fixed to one place. There are alfo fome few of them in the jurifdiction of Cordova, on the Rivers Quarto, Tercero, and Segundo; but the greater part are either deftroyed by their wars with the other Puelches and the Mocovics, or have taken refuge with the Spaniards. There were formerly fome of this nation in the diftrict of Buenos-Ayres, on the rivers of Lujan and Conchas, and that of the Matanza; but they are now no more. Their Caciques were Mugeloop, Alcochoro, Galelian, and Mayu.

Of this nation fo few remain at prefent, that they are fcarce able to raife two hundred fighting men, and only make a kind of piratical war in fmall parties, except when they are affifted by their neighbours, the Picunches, Pehuenches, and Diuihets; and, even with all their auxiliaries, cannot bring into the field above five hundred men at the moft, and feldom fo many. This nation, and that of the Diuihets, are known to the Spaniards by the name of Pampas.

The Diuihets border weftwardly upon the country of the Pehuenches, from thirty five to thirty eight degrees of fouthern latitude, and extend, along the rivers Sanquel, Colorado, and Hueyque, to within about forty miles of the Cafuhati on the eaft. They are of the fame wandering difpofition with the Taluhets, and are not much more numerous, having been greatly deftroyed in their attempts to plunder the Spaniards; fometimes taking part with the Taluhets, at other times with the Pehuenches, and frequently making their excurfions alone, on the frontiers of the mountains of Cordova and Buenos-Ayres, from the Arrecife to Lujan; killing the men, taking the women and children for flaves,

and

(101)

and driving away the cattle. The Caciques of this nation, were Concalcac, Pichivele, Yahati, and Doenoyal.

These two nations subsist chiefly on the flesh of mares, which they hunt, in small companies of about thirty or forty each, in the vast plains betwixt Mendoza and Buenos-Ayres; where they often meet with large troops of Spaniards, sent out on purpose, who execute the laws of retaliation with at least equal cruelty. But this is not the only danger which they run the risk of: for if the Tehuelhets, or Chechehets, have reached the Casuhati, or the Vuulcan and Tandil, at the time when the Diuihets and Taluhets are about to retire with their booty, they continue to fall on them in their retreat (particularly in places where the length of the march obliges them to halt for some time to rest their cattle) kill all that resist, strip the rest of every thing, and carry away the plunder.

The country of the Chechehets, or People of the East, lies properly between the River Hueyque and the First Desaguadero, or River Colorado, and from thence to the Second Desaguadero, or Black River; but they are perpetually wandering about, and move their habitations, and separate, for the most trifling motives, and oftentimes from no other reason, but their natural propensity to roving. Their country abounds only in the lesser kinds of game, as hares, armadilloes, ostriches, &c. producing few or no guanacoes. When they go up to the mountains of the Tandil and the Casuhati, on account of the scarcity of horses, they are so very unskilful in hunting, &c. that they never bring back any on their return, unless their neighbours the Tehuelhets give them some, or they have the good fortune to surprise some of the parties of the Pehuenches, who generally return well provided. In other respects, they are a poor, harmless, and sincere people, and more honest than the

D d   Moluches

Moluches or the Taluhets. They are very superstitious, extremely addicted to divinations and witchcraft, and are easily deceived. They are in general a tall, stout race of people, like their neighbours the Tehuelhets; but they speak a different language. Although they are mild and humble in peace, they are bold and active in war, as the Taluhets and Diuihets have often found to their cost; but now they are reduced to a very small number, having been destroyed by the small pox. Their surviving Caciques were Sejechu and Daychaco.

The Tehuelhets, who in Europe are known by the name of Patagons, have been, through ignorance of their idiom, called Tehuelchus: for chu signifies country or abode, and not people; which is expressed by the word het, and, more to the south, by the word kunnee or kunny. These and the Chechehets are known to the Spaniards by the name of Serranos, or Mountaineers. They are split into a great many subdivisions, as the Leuvuches, or People of the River, and Calille-Het, or People of the Mountains; amongst whom are the Chulilau-cunnees, Sehuau-cunnees, and Yacanacunnees. All these, except those of the River, are called by the Moluches, Vucha-Huilliches.

The Leuvuches live on the north and south banks of the River Negro, or, as they call it, Cufu Leuvu. To the north they have a large, uninhabited country, which is quite impassable from thick woods and lakes, and marshes, which are full of thorny, strong canes, which they call fanquel. Thus all communication is shut up from the north, but by marching westward, by the foot of the Cordillera, or eastward, by the seacoast. This people seem to be composed of the Tehuelhets and Chechehets, but speak the language of the latter, with a small mixture of the Tehuel tongue.

(103)

tongue. On the eastern side, they reach to the Chechehets; on the western, they join to the Pehuenches and Huilliches; to the north, they border on the Diuihets; and, to the south, on the other Tehuelhets. Going round the great Lake Huechun Lavquen, they reach Valdivia in six days journey from Huichin. This nation seem to be the head of the Chechehets and Tehuelhets, and their Caciques, Cacapol and his son Cangapol, are a kind of petty monarchs over all the rest. When they declare war, they are immediately joined by the Chechehets, Tehuelhets, and Huilliches, and by those Pehuenches who live most to the south, a little lower than Valdivia.

Of themselves they are but few in number, it being with the greatest difficulty that they are able to raise three hundred fighting men, having been greatly lessened by the small pox which reduced the Chechehets: for, having joined that nation, they came to the plains of Buenos-Ayres in great numbers, and attacked the famous Don Gregorio Mayu Pilqui Ya, upon the Lake of the Lobos, with a strong party of Taluhets; all of whom they cut off, and then retreated to the Vuulcan: but unfortunately they carried away with them some cloaths, which a short time before had been bought at Buenos-Ayres, and were tainted with the small pox. They have likewise been very much diminished in their wars with their northern neighbours, the Picunches, Pehuenches, and Taluhets; who, combining together, sometimes come down upon them by the side of the Cordillera and surprise them. Whenever this happens, they avoid their enemies by swimming across the river, which the others are not able to do. But the children, which in the hurry and confusion of flight are left behind, fall a prey to the inhuman enemy; who cruelly butcher all they find, not
sparing

(104)

sparing even those who hang up in their cradles. These attacks however are not always so secret, but that they sometimes have advice of them, and then few escape the fury of this brave nation; and their Cacique Cacapol shews to his guests great heaps of bones, skulls, &c. of these enemies, whom he boasts to have slain. The policy of this Cacique is to maintain peace with the Spaniards, that his people may hunt with security in the vast plains of Buenos-Ayres, between the frontiers of the Matanza, Conchas, and Magdalena, and the mountains: for which reason he does not suffer the other tribes to come down lower than Lujan, to maintain peace on the southern side. Wherefore his Caciques and confederates, in the months of July, August, and September, place themselves to hunt, where they may watch the motions of their enemies; whom they often attack and destroy. On this account these Indians never made war upon the Spaniards (though extremely jealous of them) till about 1738 or 1740; when the causes of the dispute were as follows.

The Spaniards, very injudiciously, and indeed ungratefully, drove Mayu Pilqui-Ya, the only Taluhet Cacique who was their friend, to his destruction, by forcing him to retire to a distance, exposed to the enemies which he had gained by defending their territories from the rest of his countrymen and the Picunches, and too far off to receive any succours from themselves. After the death of this Cacique, a party of Taluhets and Picunches attacked the farms of the Rivers Areco and Arecife, led on by Tseucanantu and Carulonco; and the Spaniards, with their Maestre de Campo, Don Juan de St. Martin, being too late to overtake the robbers, turned to the southward, that they might not return empty-handed. Here they met with the tents of the old Caleliyan, with one

half

(105)

half of his people, who, entirely ignorant of what had happened, were sleeping without suspicion of danger. Without examining if these were the aggressors, they fired upon them while they lay asleep in their tents, and killed many of them, with their wives and children. The rest, being awakened, and beholding the sad spectacle of their slaughtered wives and children, were resolved not to survive the loss of them, and snatching up their arms, sold their lives as dearly as they could; but, in the end, they and their Cacique were all put to the sword.

The young Caleliyan was at that time absent, but having notice of what had happened, returned upon the retreat of the Spaniards, and beholding the slaughter of his father, relations, and friends, resolved on immediate vengeance; and raising about three hundred men, among his countrymen and the Picunches, fell upon the village of Lujan, killed a great number of Spaniards, took some captives, and drove away some thousands of cattle. Upon this, the Spaniards raised about six hundred of their militia, and a troop of regulars, with all expedition, but not soon enough for so swift an enemy. Not being able to overtake him, they turned round by the salt ponds, and fell down to the Casuhati, where the Cacique Cangapol was at that time, with a few Indians, who prudently retired. Being disappointed here, they returned by the sea side, towards the Vuulcan, where they met a troop of Huilliches; who, being friends and at peace, went without arms to receive them, not having the least suspicion of any danger; but by the order of the Maestre del Campo they were quickly surrounded and cut in pieces, although the military officer of the troop remonstrated against such a proceeding, and interceded in their behalf. Having performed this exploit, they marched to the Salado, not above

E e   forty

(106)

forty leagues from the city, and about twenty from the farms of Buenos-Ayres; where a Tehuel Cacique, called Tolmichi-ya, coufin to Cacapol, and the friend and ally of the Spaniards, and much refpected by them, was encamped, under the protection of the then Governor Salcedo. This Cacique, with the Governor's letter in his hand, and fhewing his licenfe, was fhot through the head by the Maeftre del Campo; all the Indian men were killed, and the women and children made captives, with the youngeft fon of the Cacique, a boy of about twelve years of age. His eldeft fon very fortunately was gone out two days before, to hunt wild horfes, with a party of Indians.

This cruel conduct of the Maeftre del Campo fo exafperated all the Indian nations of Puelches and Moluches, that they all took arms againft the Spaniards; who found themfelves attacked at once, from the frontiers of Cordova and Santa Fe, down the whole length of the River of Plate, on a frontier of a hundred leagues; and in fuch a manner, that it was impoffible to defend themfelves: for the Indians, in fmall flying parties, falling on many villages or farms at the fame time, and generally by moon-light, it was impoffible to tell the numbers of their parties; fo that while the Spaniards purfued them in great numbers on one part, they left all the reft unguarded.

Cacapol, who, with his Tehuelhets, as yet had lived in friendfhip with the Spaniards, was highly irritated at the attempt made on his fon, the flaughter of his friends the Huilliches, the murder of his beft-beloved kinfman and other relations, and the unworthy manner in which their dead bodies had been treated; and though he was at that time near feventy years of age, he took the field at the head of a thoufand men (fome fay four thoufand) confifting of

Tehuelhets,

(107)

Tehuelhets, Huilliches, and Pehuenches, and fell upon the District of the Magdalen, about four leagues distant from Buenos-Ayres, and divided his troops with so much judgment, that he scoured and dispeopled, in one day and a night, above twelve leagues of the most populous and plentiful country in these parts. They killed many Spaniards, and took a great number of women and children captives, with above twenty thousand head of cattle, besides horses, &c. In this expedition the Indians lost only one Tehuelhet, who, straggling from the rest in hopes of plunder, fell into the hands of the Spaniards. Cangapol, the son of Cacapol, was pursued and overtaken; but the Spaniards had not the courage to attack him, though at that time double in number, both they and their horses being quite tired with their expeditious march of forty leagues, without taking any refreshment.

The inhabitants of Buenos-Ayres, having early notice from the fugitives of this unexpected attack, were in the most terrible consternation; many of the military officers ran about the streets bare-headed, in a state of distraction, and the churches and religious houses were filled with people, who had taken shelter in them, as if the enemy had been in the city. The Spaniards, humbled by this blow, deprived the Field-Marshal of his commission, and appointed another, and then raised an army of seven hundred men; which marched to the Casuhati, not to renew the war, but to sue for peace. A whole year had now elapsed since their last defeat, and the Indians, with their young Cacique Cangapol at their head, had raised another army, from all the different nations, consisting of near four thousand men; with which they might have cut all the Spaniards in pieces: yet, notwithstanding these advantages, they listened to the proposal of

the

(108)

the new Field-Marſhal, whom they conſidered as their friend; who, fearful of the conſequences which might attend a freſh rupture, offered, among other conditions, to deliver up all the Indian captives without any conſideration whatſoever, and that the Spaniſh captives ſhould be ranſomed. The indignity of this condition was ſtrongly repreſented by the Jeſuit Miſſionary, who, with ſome of his Chechehet and Tehuel Converts, went with the Spaniſh camp, and by whoſe means chiefly the Indians were prevailed upon to ſpare the Spaniſh army. He propoſed that there ſhould be a mutual exchange of priſoners; but ſo great was the fear of another war, that his advice was rejected, though many of the Indians did not deſire more honourable conditions. Some Tehuel Caciques, who had brought their captives along with them, immediately delivered them up, on making peace, not underſtanding the propoſal of the Field-Marſhal in any other light, than that the delivery of priſoners was to be reciprocal. The Moluches indeed went to Buenos-Ayres, and recovered all the Indian priſoners, as well as thoſe of the Tehuelhets, without returning the captives they had taken from the Spaniards. Since this time, the Tehuelhets, allured by the hopes of plunder, have once a year made incurſions into the territory of Buenos-Ayres, and carried away great numbers of cattle. However this was the utmoſt damage they ever did, till the year 1767; when, having received ſome provocation, they renewed the war, and carried away many captives; and of two parties of Spaniards who purſued them ten only eſcaped. A greater body of troops, with all the militia of Buenos-Ayres, and ſome companies of regulars, with their Colonel Catani, afterwards overtook them, but thought it prudent to let them go unmoleſted, for fear of ſharing the fate of their companions.

The

(109)

The Tehuelhets that border all along, from eaſt to weſt, on thoſe of the River of Sauces, are bounded on the north eaſt by the Chechehets, and on the eaſt by a vaſt deſart, which begins at about forty leagues from the mouth of the Black River towards the ſouth, and extends almoſt to the Straits of Magellan. To the weſtward, they border on the Huilliches who inhabit the ſeacoaſts of Chiloe, and extend to forty four degrees of ſouthern latitude. All their country is mountainous, with deep vallies, and has no conſiderable rivers. The natives are ſupplied with water from ſprings and ſmall rivulets, which end in lakes, where they water their cattle. In dry ſummers theſe lakes are empty, and then they are obliged to go for water to the Black River or elſewhere. This nation neither ſow nor plant, but live chiefly on guanacoes, hares, and oſtriches, which their country affords, and on mares fleſh, when they can get it.

The ſcarcity of this food occaſions them to be in perpetual motion, from one country to another, to ſeek for it : ſo that they go, in great numbers, ſometimes to the Caſuhati ; at other times, to the mountains of Vuulcan or Tandil, and the plains near Buenos-Ayres ; which is three or four hundred leagues from their own country. Of all nations upon earth, there is no account of any ſo reſtleſs, and who have ſuch a diſpoſition to roving as theſe people : for neither extreme old-age, blindneſs, nor any other diſtemper, prevents them from indulging this inclination to wander. They are a very ſtrong, well-made people, and not ſo tawny as the other Indians : ſome of their women are even as white as the Spaniards. They are courteous, obliging, and good-natured ; but very inconſtant, and not to be relied on in their promiſes and engagements. They are ſtout, warlike, and fearleſs of death. They are by much the moſt numerous of all

F f the

(110)

the Indian nations of thefe parts, and are as many as all the reft put together. They are the enemies of the Moluches, and extremely feared by them; and if they had been as well provided with horfes as the Moluches, the latter, who are fo terrible to the Spaniards, would have been long fince deftroyed; nor would the Diuihets and Taluhets have been able to have withftood their power.

To the fouth of thefe live the Chulilau-cunnees and Sehuau-cunnees, which are the moft fouthern Indians who ride on horfeback. Sehuau fignifies, in the Tehuel dialect, a fpecies of black rabbit, about the fize of a field-rat; and as their country abounds in thefe animals, their name may be derived from thence; cunnee fignifying people.

The two laft-mentioned nations appear to be the fame people with the other Tehuelhets, and differ little in their idiom. The fmall difference there is may be owing to the communication they have with the Poy-yus and Key-yus, who live upon the weftern coaft and the ftraits.

All the Tehuelhets fpeak a different language from the other Puelches and the Moluches, and this difference does not only include words, but alfo the declinations and conjugations of them; though they ufe fome of the words of both nations. For example, for a mountain they fay calille; the Moluches, calel; but the Puelches, cafu. Pichua is the Tehuel name for a guanaco, but has no likenefs to luhuan, or huanque, in the Molu tongue: nor yagip, water, to co: nor yagiu, watering-place, to cohue; nor cunnee, people, to che or het. I am inclined to think that thefe nations of Tehuelhets are thofe which the Miffionaries of Chili have called Poy-yus, as they live in the fituation in
which

(111)

which they place the Poy-yus: but the truth is that the Poy-yus live nearer the seacoast.

The last of the Tehuel nations are the Yacana-cunnees, which signifies foot-people; for they always travel on foot, having no horses in their country. To the north, they border on the Sehuau-cunnees; to the west, on the Key-yus, or Key-yuhues, from whom they are divided by a ridge of mountains: to the east, they are bounded by the ocean; and to the south, by the islands of Tierra del Fuego, or the South Sea. These Indians live near the sea, on both sides of the straits, and oftentimes make war with one another. They make use of light floats, like those of Chiloe, in order to pass the straits. They are sometimes attacked by the Huilliches, and the other Tehuelhets, who carry them away for slaves, as they have nothing to lose but their liberty and their lives. They live chiefly on fish; which they catch, either by diving, or striking them with their darts. They are very nimble of foot, and catch guanacoes and ostriches with their bowls. Their stature is much the same as that of the other Tehuelhets, rarely exceeding seven feet, and oftentimes not six feet. They are an innocent, harmless people.

When the French or Spaniards go (as they frequently do) to the Tierra del Fuego, to get fuel for the Malouin settlements, these people give them all the assistance in their power. To invite them down, they always make use of a white flag, that they may be known; for such impressions have they received of the English, that on seeing a red flag they always run away. The French and Spaniards attribute this to some English vessels having fired some great guns; the report of which, they suppose, frightened the Indians to such a degree, that they never dared to appear

since

(112)

fince, on feeing the red colours. This may have been the cafe; but it is certain many artifices have been made ufe of, to prevent their having any communication with the Englifh. A Cacique of this nation, who came with the other Tehuelhets to pay me a vifit, told me that he had been in a houfe of wood, that travelled on the water. As this was told me a few years after Admiral Anfon paffed to the South Sea, I concluded it might be one of the fhips belonging to his fquadron.

All thefe nations of the Tehuelhets are called, by the Moluches, Vucha-Huilliches, or Great Southern People: the Spaniards call them Mountaineers, though they are ignorant from whence they come. To the reft of Europe they are known by the name of Patagonians.

As I mentioned in the introduction, I have feen Caciques of all the different nations of Indians inhabiting the fouthern part of America, and obferved that the Puelches, or Eaftern Indians, were a large race of people, and feveral of them near feven feet fix inches high : but thefe are not a diftinct race; for I have feen others, of the fame family, who were not above fix feet high. The Moluches, or Weftern Indians, who live among the mountains, are rather of low ftature, but broad and thick-fet. The inhabitants of the foggy mountains of the Cordillera are often guilty of fuicide; a crime feldom heard of among the Eaftern Indians.

The names of their Caciques which I knew, were Cacapol, Cangapol, Yampalco, Tolmichiya, Guelmen, Saufimiyan, Yepelche, Marique, Chuyuentuya, Guerquen, Clufgell, Millarfuel, and Tamu.

The report that there is a nation in thefe parts defcended from Europeans, or the remains of fhipwrecks, is, I verily believe, entirely falfe and groundlefs, and occafioned by mifunderftanding

(113)

understanding the accounts of the Indians. For if they are asked in Chili concerning any inland settlement of Spaniards, they give an account of towns and white people, meaning Buenos-Ayres, &c. and so vice versa; not having the least idea, that the inhabitants of these two distant countries are known to each other. Upon my questioning the Indians on this subject, I found my conjecture to be right; and they acknowledged, upon my naming Chiloe, Valdivia, &c. (at which they seemed amazed) that those were the places they had mentioned under the description of European settlements.

What further makes this settlement of the Cæsares to be altogether incredible, is the moral impossibility that even two or three hundred Europeans, almost all men, without having any communication with a civilized country, could penetrate through so many warlike and numerous nations, and maintain themselves as a separate republic, in a country which produces nothing spontaneously, and where the inhabitants live only by hunting; and all this for the space of two hundred years (as the story is told) without being extirpated, either by being killed, or made slaves by the Indians, or without losing all European appearances by intermarrying with them. And besides, there is not a foot of all this continent, that the wandering nations do not ramble over every year; for even the uninhabited desart, which is washed by the Atlantic Ocean, is travelled over every year, to bury the dry bones of the dead, and to look for salt. Their Caciques, and others of the greatest repute for truth among them, have often protested to me, that there are no white people in all those parts, except those which are known to all Europe; as in Chili, Buenos-Ayres, Chiloe, Mendoza, &c.

G g   CHAPTER

CHAPTER V.

The Religion, Government, Policy, and Customs, of the Moluches and Puelches.

THESE Indians believe in two superior beings, the one good, the other evil. The good power is called by the Moluches Toquichen, which signifies governor of the people; by the Taluhets and Diuihets, Soychu, which, in their tongue, signifies the being who presides in the land of strong drink: the Tehuelhets call him Guayava-cunnee, or the lord of the dead.

They have formed a multiplicity of these deities; each of whom they believe to preside over one particular cast or family of Indians, of which he is supposed to have been the creator. Some make themselves of the cast of the tiger, some of the lion, some of the guanaco, and others of the ostrich, &c. They imagine that these deities have each their separate habitations, in vast caverns under the earth, beneath some lake, hill, &c. and that when an Indian dies, his soul goes to live with the deity who presides over his particular family, there to enjoy the happiness of being eternally drunk.

They believe that their good deities made the world, and that they first created the Indians in their caves, gave them the lance, the bow and arrows, and the stone-bowls, to fight and hunt with, and then turned them out to shift for themselves.

(115)

felves. They imagine that the deities of the Spaniards did the fame by them, but that inftead of lances, bows, &c. they gave them guns and fwords. They fuppofe that when the beafts, birds, and leffer animals were created, thofe of the more nimble kind came immediately out of their caves, but that the bulls and cows being the laft, the Indians were fo frightened at the fight of their horns, that they ftopped up the entrance of their caves with great ftones. This is the reafon they give, why they had no black cattle in their country, till the Spaniards brought them over, who more wifely had let them out of the caves.

They have formed a belief that fome of them after death are to return to thefe divine caverns; and they fay alfo that the ftars are old Indians, that the milky way is the field where the old Indians hunt oftriches, and that the two fouthern clouds are the feathers of the oftriches which they kill. They have an opinion alfo that the creation is not yet exhaufted, nor all of it come out to the daylight of this upper world.

Their wizards, beating their drums, and rattling their cala-bafhes full of fea-fhells, pretend to fee, under ground, men, cattle, &c. with fhops of rum, brandy, cafcabels, and a va-riety of other things. But I am very well affured that they do not all of them believe this nonfenfe: for the Tehuel Cacique, Chehuentuya, came to me one morning, with an account of a new difcovery, made by one of their wizards, of one of thefe fubterraneous countries, which was under the place where we lived; and upon my laughing at, and expofing their fimplicity, in being impofed upon by fuch fables and foolifh ftories, he anfwered with fcorn, Epu-cungeing'n, They are old women's tales.

The Evil Principle is called by the Moluches Huecuvoe, or Huecuvu, that is, the Wanderer without. The Tehu-

clhets

(116)

elhets and Checheliets call him Atſkannakanatz ; the other Puelches call him Valichu.

They acknowledge a great number of this kind of demons, wandering about the world, and attribute to them all the evil that is done in it, whether to man or beaſt ; and they carry this opinion ſo far, as to believe that theſe unpropitious powers occaſion the wearineſs and fatigue which attends long journeys or hard labour. Each of their wizards is ſuppoſed to have two of theſe demons in conſtant attendance, who enable them to foretel future events ; to diſcover what is paſſing, at the time preſent, at a great diſtance ; and to cure the ſick, by fighting, driving away, or appeaſing, the other demons who torment them. They believe that the ſouls of their wizards, after death, are of the number of theſe demons.

Their worſhip is entirely directed to the evil being, except in ſome particular ceremonies made uſe of in reverence to the dead. To perform their worſhip, they aſſemble together in the tent of the wizard ; who is ſhut up from the ſight of the reſt, in a corner of the tent. In this apartment, he has a ſmall drum, one or two round calabaſhes with ſmall ſea-ſhells in them, and ſome ſquare bags of painted hide, in which he keeps his ſpells. He begins the ceremony, by making a ſtrange noiſe with his drum and rattle-box; after which he feigns a fit, or ſtruggle with the devil, who it is then ſuppoſed has entered into him; keeps his eyes lifted up, diſtorts the features of his face, foams at the mouth, ſcrews up his joints, and, after many violent and diſtorting motions, remains ſtiff and motionleſs, reſembling a man ſeized with an epilepſy. After ſome time he comes to himſelf, as having got the better of the demon ; next feigns, within his tabernacle, a faint, ſhrill, mournful voice, as of the evil ſpirit, who, by this diſmal cry, is ſuppoſed to

acknowledge

(117)

acknowledge himfelf fubdued; and then, from a kind of tripod, anfwers all queftions that are put to him. Whether his anfwers be true or falfe is of no great fignification; becaufe if his intelligence fhould prove falfe, it is the fault of the devil. On all thefe occafions the wizard is well paid.

The profeffion of the wizards is very dangerous, notwithftanding the refpect which is fometimes paid to them: for it often happens, when an Indian Chief dies, that fome of the wizards are killed; efpecially if they had any difpute with the deceafed juft before his death; the Indians, in this cafe, laying the lofs of their Chief upon the wizards and their demons. In cafes alfo of peftilence and epidemic diforders, when great numbers are carried off, the wizards often fuffer. On account of the fmallpox, which happened after the death of Mayu Pilqui-ya and his people, and almoft entirely deftroyed the Chechehets, Cangapol ordered all the wizards to be killed, to fee if by thefe means the diftemper would ceafe.

The wizards are of both fexes. The male wizards are obliged (as it were) to leave their fex, and to drefs themfelves in female apparel, and are not permitted to marry, though the female ones or witches may. They are generally chofen for this office when they are children, and a preference is always fhewn to thofe, who at that early time of life difcover an effeminate difpofition. They are cloathed very early in female attire, and prefented with the drum and rattles belonging to the profeffion they are to follow.

They who are feized with fits of the falling ficknefs, or the chorea Sancti Viti, are immediately felected for this employment, as chofen by the demons themfelves; whom they fuppofe to poffefs them, and to caufe all thofe convulfions and diftortions common in epileptic paroxyfms.

H h   The

(118)

The burial of their dead, and the fuperftitious reverence paid to their memory, are attended with great ceremony. When an Indian dies, one of the moft diftinguifhed women among them is immediately chofen, to make a fkeleton of his body; which is done, by cutting out the entrails, which they burn to afhes, diffecting the flefh from the bones as clean as poffible, and then burying them under ground, till the remaining flefh is entirely rotted off, or till they are re-moved (which muft be within a year after the interment, but is fometimes within two months) to the proper burial-place of their anceftors.

This cuftom is ftrictly obferved by the Moluches, Taluhets, and Diuihets; but the Chechehets and Tehuelhets, or Pata-gonians, place the bones on high, upon canes or twigs woven together, to dry and whiten with the fun and rain.

During the time that the ceremony of making the fkele-ton lafts, the Indians, covered with long mantles of fkins, and their faces blackened with foot, walk round the tent, with long poles or lances in their hands; finging in a mourn-ful tone of voice, and ftriking the ground, to frighten away the Valichus or Evil Beings. Some go to vifit and confole the widow, or widows, and other relations of the dead; that is, if there is any thing to be got; for nothing is done, but with a view of intereft. During this vifit of condolance, they cry, howl, and fing, in the moft difmal manner; ftrain-ing out tears, and pricking their arms and thighs with fharp thorns, to make them bleed. For this fhow of grief they are paid with glafs beads, brafs cafcabels, and fuch like bawbles, which are in high eftimation among them. The horfes of the dead are alfo immediately killed, that he may have wherewithal to ride upon in the Alhue Mapu, or Country of the Dead; referving only a few, to grace

the

(119)

the laſt funeral pomp, and to carry the relicks to their proper ſepulchres.

The widow, or widows, of the dead, are obliged to mourn
and faſt for a whole year after the death of their huſband.
This conſiſts, in keeping themſelves cloſe ſhut up in their
tents, without having communication with any one, or ſtirring
out, but for the common neceſſaries of life; in not waſhing
their faces or hands, but being blackened with ſoot, and
having their garments of a mournful appearance; in ab-
ſtaining from horſe's and cow's fleſh, and, within-land, where
they are plenty, from the fleſh of oſtriches and guanacoes; but
they may eat any thing elſe. During the year of mourning
they are forbidden to marry, and if, within this time, a widow is diſcovered to have had any communication with a
man, the relations of her dead huſband will kill them both;
unleſs it appears that ſhe has been violated. But I did not
diſcover that the men were obliged to any ſuch kind of
mourning on the death of their wives.

When they remove the bones of their dead, they pack
them up together in a hide, and place them upon one of
the deceaſed's favourite horſes, kept alive for that purpoſe;
which they adorn after their beſt faſhion, with mantles,
feathers, &c. and travel in this manner, though it be to the
diſtance of three hundred leagues, till they arrive at the
proper burial-place, where they perform the laſt ceremony.

The Moluches, Taluhets, and Diuihets, bury their dead
in large ſquare pits, about a fathom deep. The bones are
put together, and ſecured by tying each in their proper place,
then cloathed with the beſt robes they can get, adorned with
beads, plumes, &c. all of which they cleanſe or change once a
year. They are placed in a row, ſitting, with the ſword, lance,
bow and arrows, bowls, and whatever elſe the deceaſed had.

while

(120)

while alive. Thefe pits are covered over with beams or trees, canes, or twigs woven together, upon which they put earth. An old matron is chofen out of each tribe, to take care of thefe graves, and on account of her employment is held in great veneration. Her office is, to open every year thefe dreary habitations, and to cloath and clean the fkeletons. Befides all this, they every year pour upon thefe graves fome bowls of their firft-made chica, and drink fome of it themfelves to the good health of the dead. Thefe burying places are, in general, not far diftant from their ordinary habitations; and they place all around the bodies of their dead horfes, raifed upon their feet, and fupported with fticks.

The Tehuelhets, or more fouthern Patagonians, differ in fome refpects from the other Indians. After having dried the bones of their dead, they carry them to a great diftance from their habitations, into the defert by the feacoaft, and after placing them in their proper form, and adorning them in the manner before defcribed, they fet them in order above ground, under a hut or tent, erected for that purpofe, with the fkeletons of their dead horfes placed around them.

In the expedition of the year 1746, fome Spanifh foldiers, with one of the miffionaries, travelling about thirty leagues within-land, to the weft of Port San Julian, found one of thefe Indian fepulchres, containing three fkeletons, and having as many dead horfes propped up round it.

It is not an eafy matter to trace any regular form of government, or civil conftitution, among thefe Indians: what little they have, feems to confift in a fmall degree of fubjection to their Caciques. The office of a Cacique is hereditary, not elective; and all the fons of a Cacique have a right to affume the dignity, if they can get any Indians to
follow

(121)

follow them; but, on account of the little use it is of to it's possessors, it is oftentimes resigned.

The Cacique has the power of protecting as many as apply to him, of composing or silencing any difference, or delivering over the offending party to be punished with death, without being accountable for it; for in these respects his will is the law. He is generally too apt to take bribes; delivering up his vassals, and even his relations, when well paid for it. According to his orders, the Indians encamp, march, or travel from one place to another, to settle, hunt, or make war. He frequently summons them to his tent, and harangues them upon their behaviour, the exigencies of the time, the injuries they have received, the measures to be taken, &c. In these harangues, he always extols his own prowess and personal merit. When he is eloquent, he is greatly esteemed; and when a Cacique is not endowed with that accomplishment, he generally has an orator, who supplies his place. In cases of importance, especially those of war, he calls a council of the principal Indians and wizards; with whom he consults about the measures to be taken, to defend himself, or attack his enemies.

In a general war, when many nations enter into an alliance against a common enemy, they choose an Apo, or Commander in Chief, from among the oldest or most celebrated of the Caciques. But this honour, though elective, has for many years been in a manner hereditary, among those of the south, in the family of Cangapol; who leads the Tehuelhets, Chechehets, Huilliches, Pehuenches, and Diuihets, when they join their forces together. They generally encamp at about thirty or forty leagues distance from the enemies country, that they may not be discovered, and send out scouts, to examine the places they intend to attack; who hide them-

I i   selves

(122)

felves during the day, but at night iffue forth from their lurking places, and mark, with the greateft exactnefs, every houfe and farm of the ftraggling villages they intend to attack, fo as to give an account of their difpofition, the number of their inhabitants, and their means of defence. When they have thus informed themfelves, they communicate the intelligence to the main army, who take the time when the moon is paft the full, that they may have light for their work, to march to the affault. When they approach the place, they feparate in fmall bodies, each of which is appointed to attack fome houfe or farm. A few hours after midnight they make the affault, kill all the men who refift, and carry away the women and children for flaves. The Indian women follow their hufbands, armed with clubs, bowls, and fometimes fwords; and ravage and plunder the houfes of every thing they can find, that may be of fervice to them, as cloaths, houfhold utenfils, &c. Thus loaded with booty, they retire as faft as they can; refting neither day nor night, till they are at a great diftance, and out of danger of being overtaken by their enemies; which is fometimes a hundred leagues from the place of the attack. Here they ftop, and divide their booty; which is feldom accomplifhed without great difcontents from fome or other of them, and thefe often terminate in quarrels and bloodfhed.

At other times, they make a kind of flying war, with fmall camps, of fifty or a hundred men in each. In this cafe they do not attack whole villages, but only fingle farms or houfes, which they do very haftily, and retire as foon as they can.

The Caciques neverthelefs have not the power to raife taxes, nor to take away any thing from their vaffals; nor can they oblige them to ferve in the leaft employment, without

paying

(123)

paying them. On the contrary, they are obliged to treat their vaffals with great humanity and mildnefs, and oftentimes to relieve their wants, or they will feek the protection of fome other Cacique. For this reafon, many of the Elmens, or thofe who are born Caciques, refufe to have any vaffals; as they coft them dear, and yield but little profit. No Indian, or body of Indians, can live without the protection of fome Cacique, according to their law of nations; and if any of them attempted to do it, they would undoubtedly be killed, or carried away as flaves, as foon as they were difcovered.

In cafe of any injury, notwithftanding the authority of the Cacique, the party aggrieved often endeavours to do himfelf juftice to the beft of his power. They know of no punifhment, or fatisfaction, but that of paying, or redeeming the injury, or damage done, with fomething of value in their eftimation (for they ufe no money) nor do they chaftize, but by death. Yet when the offence is not very great, and the offender is poor, the party injured generally beats him with his ftone bowls, on the back and ribs. When the offender is too powerful, they let him alone; unlefs the Cacique interferes, and obliges him to make fatisfaction.

Their wars, in which the different nations engage one with another, and alfo with the Spaniards, arife fometimes from injuries received, which they are eager to revenge; but often from want of provifions, or a defire of plunder.

Although the different nations are at continual variance among themfelves, yet they often join together againft the Spaniards, and choofe an Apo, or Captain-general, to command the whole: at other times, each nation makes war for itfelf. In the wars with the Spaniards of Buenos-Ayres, the Moluches are as auxiliaries, and the Chiefs are chofen from

among

(124)

among the Puelches, becaufe they are better acquainted with that country. For the like reafon, in the wars with the Spaniards of Chili, the Chiefs are elected from among the Caciques of the Moluches.

Their marriages are made by fale; the hufband buying his wife of her neareft relations, and oftentimes at a dear price, of beads, cafcabels, garments, horfes, or any thing elfe that is of value among them. They often agree for their wives, and pay part of the price for them, when they are very young, and many years before they are marriageable. Each Indian may have as many wives as he can buy or keep. Widows and orphans are at their own difpofal, and may accept of whom they pleafe: the reft are obliged to abide by the fale, even againft their inclinations, or they are dragged away and compelled to fubmit. It feldom happens that any Indian has more than one wife; though fome have had two or three at a time; efpecially the Elmens, Yas, or Caciques. The reafon of this is, that they are not overftocked with women; and thofe which they have are fo dear, that many have no wife at all.

They ufe little or no ceremony in their marriages. At the time agreed upon, the parents lead the lady to the fpoufe's habitation, and deliver her up to him; or he goes and takes her away from her parents, as his own property; and fometimes fhe even goes of herfelf, being certain of a good reception. The following morning fhe is vifited by her relations, before the time of rifing; and being found in bed with her fpoufe, the marriage is concluded. But as many of thefe marriages are compulfive on the fide of the woman, they are frequently fruftrated. The contumacy of the woman fometimes tires out the patience of the man, who then turns her away, or fells her to the perfon on whom fhe has fixed her affections;

(125)

affections; but seldom beats her, or treats her ill. At other times the wife elopes from her husband, and goes to a gallant; who, if he is more powerful, or of a higher rank than the husband, obliges him to put up with the affront, and to acquiesce in the loss of his wife; unless a more powerful friend obliges the gallant to a restitution, or to compound the matter; and in these affairs they are generally very easy.

The women, who have once accepted their husbands, are in general very faithful and laborious. Indeed their lives are but one continued scene of labour; for, besides the nursing and bringing up their children, they are obliged to submit to every species of drudgery. In short they do every thing, except hunting and fighting; and sometimes they even engage in the latter. The care of all houshold affairs is left entirely to the women: they fetch wood and water, dress victuals, make, mend, and clean the tents, dress and few together the hides, and also the lesser skins of which they make their mantles or carapas, and spin and make ponchas or macuns. When they travel, the women pack up every thing, even the tent-poles; which they must erect and pull down themselves, as often as occasion requires: they load, unload, and settle the baggage, straiten the girths of the saddles, and carry the lance before their husbands. No excuse of sickness, or being big with child, will relieve them from the appointed labour: and so rigidly are they obliged to perform their duty, that their husbands cannot help them on any occasion, or in the greatest distress, without incurring the highest ignominy. The women of quality, or those related to the Caciques, are permitted to have slaves, who ease their mistresses of the most laborious part of their work; but if they should not have any slaves, they must undergo the same fatigue as the rest.

K k

It

(126)

It is the province of the hufband to provide food; which is generally the flefh of horfes, oftriches, guanacoes, hares, wild-boars, armadilloes, antas, &c. or whatever the country produces. He alfo fupplies his wife with fkins for the tent, and for cloathing; though they often purchafe for them cloaths or mantles of European goods, of the Spaniards; and alfo brafs-earings, cafcabels, and large glafs beads of a fky-blue colour, for which they have a great preference. I have feen them exchange a poncha, or mantle, of their little foxes fkins, which are as fine and as beautiful as ermine, worth from five to feven dollars each, for four ftrings of thefe beads, which are worth about fourpence. The Moluches maintain fome flocks of fheep for their wool, and fow a fmall quantity of corn: but the Puelches depend entirely on their hunting; for which purpofe they keep great numbers of dogs, which they call tehua.

Although their marriages are at will, yet when once the parties are agreed, and have children, they feldom forfake each other; even in extreme old-age. The hufband protects his wife from all injuries, and always takes her part, even if fhe is in the wrong; which occafions frequent quarrels and bloodfhed: but this partiality does not prevent him from reprimanding her in private, for engaging him in thefe difputes. He feldom beats her; and if he catches her in any criminal commerce, lays all the blame on the gallant; whom he corrects with great feverity, unlefs he atones for the injury by fome valuable prefent. They have fo little decency in this refpect, that oftentimes, at the command of the wizards, they, fuperftitioufly fend their wives to the woods, to proftitute themfelves to the firft perfon they meet. Yet there are fome women whofe modefty gets the better of their obedience, and who

(127)

who refuse to fulfil the desires both of their husbands and the wizards.

They breed up their children in a vicious indulgence of their humours. The Tehuelhets, or Southern Patagonians, carry this folly to the greatest excess; and the old people are led about from one place to another, frequently changing their habitations, to humour the caprices of their children. The following account may give an idea, to what a degree of folly they carry this fondness. If an Indian, even a Cacique, resolve to change his habitation, with his family, &c. and is at that time an inhabitant among a different tribe of people, who do not choose to part with him, it is the custom to take one of his children, and to pretend such a fondness for it, that they cannot part with it; and by these means the father is satisfied, and agrees to stay: they then deliver him his child, and, instead of resenting their conduct, he is greatly pleased that his child is so much beloved.

The widow of a Tehuel Cacique, whose husband had been treacherously killed by the Spaniards in time of peace, was determined to leave the town and the missionaries, and no entreaties or persuasions were able to quiet her on so sad an occasion. She had a son about six years of age, who was very fond of the missionaries, on account of the presents of bread, figs, raisins, &c. which they used to give him; and when he understood that his mother was preparing to carry him away, he would not suffer himself to be dressed for the journey, and desired to be carried to the fathers. The mother, moved with the distress of her child, consented to remain where she was, and soon afterwards became a Christian.

The dress of these Indians is very remarkable. The men wear no caps upon their heads, but have their hair tied up

behind

(128)

behind, with the points upwards; binding it many times above the head with a large girdle of dyed woollen stuff, curiously wrought. In their tents they wear a mantle, made of skins sewed together. Those made with the skins of young colts and mares are the least valuable. The mantles made of the skins of a small, stinking animal, like our pole-cat, which they call yaguane, are superior to these last. This animal is of a dark, sable colour, with two large white streaks on each side of it's ribs; it's hair very soft and fine.

The fur of the coipu, or otter, is in equal esteem with that of the yaguane, or maikel. The head, mouth and teeth of this animal very much resemble those of a rabbit: it's fur is long and fine, and as good as that of a beaver. It digs it's caves (which consist of one or two stories) in the banks of rivers, and lives upon fish. It has a long, round, tapering tail, like that of a rat; and it's flesh is very good to eat.

The mantles made of the skins of guanacoes are in still greater estimation than those before-mentioned, on account of the warmth and fineness of their wool, and their long duration. But those which are in the highest esteem of all are made with the skins of small foxes, which are exceedingly soft and beautiful. They are of a mottled grey, with a red cast, but not so durable as those of the guanaco.

They also make or weave (the Tehuelhets and Chechehets excepted) fine mantles of woollen yarn, beautifully dyed with many colours; which when wrapped round their bodies, reach from their shoulders to the calf of the leg. They have another, of the same kind, round the waist, and, besides these, a small three-cornered leathern apron, that serves for breeches. They tie two corners of it round their waists, and pass the other between their legs, and fasten it
behind.

(129)

behind. They likewife make mantles of red ftuffs, fuch as everlafting, &c. which they buy of the Spaniards; as alfo hats, which they are fond of wearing, efpecially on horfe-back. They adorn themfelves with fky-coloured beads; tying one or two rows of them round their necks and wrifts. They alfo paint their faces, fometimes with red, at other times with black; making themfelves exceedingly ugly and hideous, though they imagine there is great beauty in it.

When they are on horfeback, inftead of the mantle be-fore-mentioned, they ufe one adorned with a greater variety of figures; which has a flit in the middle, through which they put their heads; and the mantle hangs down to their knees, and fometimes to their feet. Both men and women ufe a kind of boots or ftockings, made of the fkin of the thighs and legs of mares and colts; which they firft flay from the fat and inward membranes, and, after drying, foften with greafe; then make them pliant by wringing, and put them on without either fhaping or fewing.

Their defenfive arms confift of a helmet, made like a broad-brimmed hat, of a bull's hide fewed double, and of a coat of mail; which is a wide tunic, fhaped and put on like a fhirt, with narrow fhort fleeves, made of three or four folds of the anta's fkin. It is very heavy, ftrong enough to refift either arrows or lances; and fome fay it is bullet-proof. It is made very high in the neck-part, and almoft covers the eyes and nofe. On foot they ufe likewife a large, un-wieldy, fquare target, of bulls hides. Their offenfive arms are a fhort bow, and arrows pointed with bone. The Te-huelhets and Huilliohes fometimes envenom the points, with a fpecies of poifon, which deftroys fo flowly, that the wound-ed perfon lingers for two or three months; till, reduced to a fkeleton, he at laft expires. They likewife ufe a lance, of

L 1   four

(130)

four or five yards in length, made of a folid cane, that grows near the Cordillera, with many joints, about four or five inches from one another, and pointed with iron. They have fwords, when they can get them from the Spaniards; but they are in general very fcarce. Another fort of weapons, peculiar to this nation, are bowls, or large, round ftones, fhaped into that form by being beat againft each other, and about four inches in diameter. They are in general pebbles, though I have feen fome, which were brought from within land, that were made of a kind of ore, refembling a fine, light copper. There are others made of a kind of iron-ftone.

Thefe bowls are of two or three forts. That which is moft ufed in war is a fingle, round bowl, of about a pound weight, to which they faften a fmall rope, made of hide or finews. With this they ftrike the adverfary's head, to dafh out his brains; and fometimes throw it, rope and all.

There is another kind, which is indifferently ufed either in war or hunting. This confifts of two bowls, like the former, covered with fkin, and faftened at each end of a long rope of hide, three or four yards in length. They take one of them in their hand, and whirling the other three or four times round their head, throw it, and entangle either man or beaft. They will throw them with fuch dexterity, as to faften a man to his horfe; and will alfo contrive to throw them in fuch a manner, when they are hunting, that the rope fhall twift round the neck of the beaft, and the bowls hang between his legs, fo that he is foon thrown down and taken.

Sometimes, efpecially in hunting, they ufe two leffer bowls, which they faften, with two ropes of about a yard each, to the rope to which the larger ones are tied, that they may entangle their prey the better. In hunting oftriches, deer, or guanacoes, they ufe bowls of a fmaller fize than any

I have

(131)

I have yet mentioned. Thefe are made of marble, well poliſhed, and faſtened to a cord made of ſinews.

The women have no attire for their heads, but have their long hair plaited in two large treſſes, which hang down on either ſide. They wear ear-rings, or pendants, of ſquare braſs plates, about two or three inches broad, and as many deep, with a piece of the fame metal well hammered to prevent their ears, which are very widely bored, from being cut. They wear ſtrings of ſky-blue beads round their necks, arms, and ankles.

They have the fame kind of mantle as the men; but they put one end of it round their necks, faſtening it before with a braſs ſkewer or pin, and gather it up round the waiſt; letting it fall down to their ankles. They have alfo a ſhort apron, tied about their middle under the mantle, which covers them only before, and reaches a little below the knee. This is woven of dyed yarn, and ſtriped from the top to the bottom with different colours. When they ride, they uſe a ſtraw hat, of the figure of a broad, low cone; ſuch as the Chineſe are repreſented to wear: and their boots are the fame as thoſe which are worn by the men.

CHAPTER

CHAPTER VI.

An Account of the Language of the Inhabitants of these Countries.

THE languages of these Indians differ from each other. I only learned that of the Moluches; it being the most polished, and the most generally understood. A considerable absence from these countries has rendered the recollection very difficult: however, I shall give the best account of it I am able, to satisfy the curious and inquisitive.

This language is much more copious and elegant, than could have been expected from an uncivilized people.

The nouns have only one declination, and are all of the common gender. The dative, accusative, and ablative cases, have all the same termination, with their suffix or postposition. There are but two numbers, singular and plural; the dual being expressed by placing the word epu (which signifies two) before the word: but the pronouns have all the three numbers. The adjectives are put before the substantives, and do not vary their terminations, either in case or number: as,

Cume   *good,*
Cume huentu   *a good man,*
Cume huentu eng'n   *good men.*

The

(133)

The Declination of the Nouns.

Singular.		Plural.	
N. Huentu,	*the man,*	N. Pu huentu or huentu eng'n	*the men,*
G. Huentuni,	*of the man,* &c.		
D. Huentumo,		G. Pu huentu, *of the men.*	
A. Huentumo,		and fo on, as in the fingular.	
V. Huentu,			
A. Huentumo,			
or Huentu engu,			

The Pronouns.

Inche,	*I,*	Quifu,	*he alone or himjelf,*
Eimi,	*thou,*		
Vei,	*he,*	Inche quifu,	*I myfelf,*
T'va or T'vachi,	*this,*	Inchiu,	*we two,*
Velli,	*that,*	Inchin,	*we many.*
Inei,	*whom,*		

And in the fame manner,

Eimi,	*thou,*	Eim'n	*you many.*
Eimu,	*you two,*		

For pronouns poffeffive is ufed the genitive, or fign of the genitive, of the pronouns; ni, mine; mi, thine. Likewife m'ten, only; ufed fometimes as an adjective or pronoun, and at other times as an adverb.

The verbs have only one conjugation, and are never irregular or defective. They are formed from any part of fpeech, either by giving it the termination of a verb, or adding to it the verb fubftantive gen, or, as it is pronounced, 'ngen, which anfwers to the Latin verb fum, es, fui, &c.

M m   EXAMPLES.

(134)

EXAMPLES.

1. P'lle,   *near,*
   P'llen *or* P'llengen,   *I am near,*
   P'lley *or* P'llengey,   *he is near.*

2. Cume,   *good,*
   Cumen,
   Cumengen,   } *to be good.*
   Cumelen,

3. Ata,   *Evil* or *bad,*
   Atan,
   Atangen,   } *to be bad,*
   Atal'n *or* Atalcan,   *to corrupt* or *make bad.*

The verbs have three numbers, fingular, dual, and plural; and as many tenfes as in the Greek tongue; all of which they form by interpofing certain particles before the laft letter of the indicative, and before the laft fyllable of the fubjunctive: as,

Prefent tenfe,	Elun,	*to give.*
Imperfect,	Elubun,	
Perfect,	Eluyeen,	
Preterperfect,	Eluyeebun,	
Firft Aorift,	Eluabun,	
Second Aorift,	Eluyeabun,	
Firft Future,	Eluan,	
Second Future,	Eluyean.	

In the fubjunctive mood they terminate with the particle li, ftriking off the letter n in the indicative, and varying all the tenfes as before: as,

Prefent

(135)

Prefent tenfe,	Eluli,
Imperfect,	Elubuli,
Perfect,	Eluyeeli,
Preterperfect,	Eluyeebuli,
Firft Aorift,	Eluabuli,
Second Aorift,	Eluyeabuli,
Firft Future,	Eluali,
Second Future,	Eluyeali.

N. B. The Huilliches frequently ufe, inftead of eluyeen, in the perfect tenfe of the indicative, or eluyeeli, in that of the fubjunctive, eluvin and eluvili.

I remarked that, for the imperative, they frequently ufed the future of the indicative, and fometimes in the third perfon; as, Elupe, *Let him give.*

A Moluche Indian, eating an oftrich's egg, and wanting falt, I heard him fay, " Chafimota iloavinquin," *Let me eat it with falt.* Now iloavin is the firft future, with the particle vi interpofed, to fignify *it.* I do not know whether quin is anything more than a particle of ornament; as in the word chafimota; where the concluding fyllable ta is ufelefs, but for the fake of the found; as chafimo, without any addition, is the ablative cafe of chafi, *falt.*

The tenfes are conjugated, through, all their numbers, with thefe terminations in the indicative prefent;

Sing.	n	imi	y
Dual	iu	imu	ingu
Plural	in	im'n	ing'n

EXAMPLE.

Sing.	Elun	Eluimi	Eluy
Dual	Eluiu	Eluimu	Eluingu
Plural	Eluin	Eluim'n	Eluing'n.

In

(136)

In the SUBJUNCTIVE.

Sing.	li	limi	liy.
Dual	liu	limu	lingu.
Plural	liin	lim'n	ling'n.

E X A M P L E.

Sing.	Eluli	Elulimi	Eluliy.
Dual	Eluliu	Elulimu	Elulingu.
Plural	Eluliin	Elulim'n	Eluling'n.

In this manner all the other tenses are conjugated.

N. B. The Second Aorift and the Second Future are only used by the Picunches, and not by the Huilliches.

The infinitive mood is formed of the firft perfon of the indicative, with the genitive of the primitive pronoun put before, or a poffeffive pronoun, to fignify the perfon that acts or fuffers, and may be taken from any of the tenfes: as,

Ni elun,	*I to give,*
Ni Elubun,	*thou to give,*
Ni Eluvin, &c.	*he to give.*

The other poffeffives are mi, thine; and 'n, his; for thefe are only ufed in the fingular.

There are two participles, formed in the fame manner as the infinitive, to be conjugated through all the tenfes; the one active, the other paffive:

| Active, | Elulu, | *the perfon giving.* |
| Paffive, | Eluel, | *the thing given.* |

From

(137)

From thefe are derived,

Elubulu,	*he that did give,*
Eluyelu,	*he that has given,*
Elualu,	*he that will give,*
Eluabulu,	*he that was to give,*
Elubuel,	*the thing that was given,*
Eluyeel,	*the thing that has been given,*
Elual, &c.	*the thing that will be given.*

Of all thefe, and of the active verbs, paffives are formed, by adding the verb fubftantive, gen; in which cafe, in all the tenfes, the variation or declenfion changes the verb fubftantive, the adjective verb remaining invariable.

E X A M P L E.

Elugen,	*I have given,*
Elugebun,	*I was given,*
Elugeli,	*I can be given,*
Elungeuyeeli,	*I may have been given,*
Elungeali, &c.	*I shall have been given.*

Another accident, which the verbs in this language fuffer, is that of tranfition: whereby they fignify, as well the perfon that acts, as him on whom the action paffes, by the interpofition or addition of certain determinate particles to exprefs it. This is common to them with thofe of Peru; but the latter ufe thofe which are more difficult, and in a greater number. I do not think that the languages of the nations of the Puelches, of the Chaco, or the Guaranies, have this particular property. I do not believe I can recollect them all; but I fhall endeavour to give the beft account I can of thefe tranfitions.

N n   The

(138)

The tranfitions are fix in number;

From *me* to *thee* or *you,*
From *you* to *me,*
From *him* to *me,*
From *him* to *you,*
From *me* or *you* to *him,*

And the mutual, when it is reciprocal on both fides.

The firft tranfition is expreffed by eymi, eymu, and eim'n, in the indicative; and elmi, elmu, and elm'n, in the fubjunctive; and this runs through all the tenfes: as,

Elun,	*I give,*
Elueymi,	*I give to you,*
Elueymu,	*I give to you two,*
Elueim'n,	*I or we give to you many.*

And in the fubjunctive,

Eluelmi,
Eluelmu,
Eluelm'n,

With their derivatives, the other tenfes.

The fecond tranfition is from *you* to *me,* and is expreffed by the particle en; as eluen, *you give to me;* which has elueiu and eluein, dual and plural.

The third tranfition from *him* to *me,* is

Sing.	Elumon,
Dual	Elumoiu,
Plural	Elumoin (*when we are many.*)

In the fubjunctive it is,

Sing.	Elumoli,
Dual	Elumoliyu,
Plural	Elumoliin.

The

(139)

The fourth tranfition, from *him* to *thee*, is formed by adding eneu to the firft perfon fingular; as,

Elueneu, *he gives to thee;*

And eymu mo, eim'n mo, to the dual and plural;

And in the fubjunctive,

Elmi mo,
Elmu mo,
Elm'n mo.

The fifth tranfition, from *me* to *thee*, to *this*, or *that*, or *him*, is formed by the interpofition of the particle vi; as,

Eluvin,	*I give it, or give him,*
Eluvimi,	*thou givefi him,*
Eluvi,	*he giveth him,*
Eluviyu, }	*we or you two give to*
Eluvimu, }	*him, or give it.*
Eluviu,	}*we many give to him, or give it.*
Eluvim'n,	

The fubjunctive is Eluvili.

This I perceive to be fomething equivocal with the perfect tenfe of the Huilliches: yet they like to ufe it, though they themfelves know the impropriety of it. Nor is this the only ground of equivocation in their tongue, which is found efpecially in the prepofitions; where one having many fignifications, the meaning is oftentimes very much confufed; as may be feen in the declination of their nouns.

The fixth and laft tranfition is conjugated through all the numbers, moods, and tenfes, in the fame manner as the fimple verbs, and is formed by the interpofition of the particle huu, or, as it is pronounced, wu; as,

Eluhuun,

(140)

Eluhuun, *or* } *I give to myself,*
Euwun,

Ayuwimi, *thou lovest thyself,*
Ayuhui, *he loveth himself,*
Ayuhuim'n,&c. *you love one another.*

They have another particular mode of compounding verbs, altering their significations, making affirmatives negatives, neuters actives, and of signifying and expressing how and in what manner the thing is done, by the interposition of prepositions, adverbs, adjectives, &c. as,

Cupan, *to come,*
Naucupan, *to come downwards.*
Nag'n, *to fall,*
Nagcumen, *to make to fall.*
Payllac'non, *to put one's mouth upwards;*

from pailla, *mouth upwards,* and c'non, *to put.*

Aucan, *to rebel,*
Aucatun, *to rebel over again,*
Aucatul'n, *to make to rebel.*
Lan, *death* or *to die,*
Langm'n, *to kill,*
Langm'chen, *to kill Indians;*

from langm'n, *to kill,* and che, *Indian or man.*

Ayun, *to love,*
Ayulan, *not to love.*

Pen signifies *to see;* pevin is *I saw him;* vemge, *on this manner;* and la is the negative. These words are compounded into one, thus, pevemgelavin, *I saw him not on this manner.*

The

(141)

The numeral words in this language are compleat, and may be ufed to defcribe any number whatfoever.

Quine,	*one,*	Meli,	*four,*	Cayu,	*fix,*
Epu,	*two,*	Kechu,	*five,*	Selge,	*feven,*
Quila,	*three,*				

Mari (*or* Maffi as the Huilliches have it) *ten,*
Pataca, *a hundred,* Huaranca, *a thoufand.*

The intermediate numbers are compofed as follows:

Maffi quine,	*eleven,*	Epu maffi epu,	*twenty two,*
Maffi epu,	*twelve,*	Epu maffi quila,	*twenty three,*
Maffi quila,	*thirteen,*	Quila pataca,	*three hundred,*
Epu maffi,	*twenty,*	Selge pataca,	*feven hundred.*

The A D V E R B S, *&c.*

Mu,	*no,*
May,	*yes,*
Chay *or* Chayula,	*to-day,* or *prefently*
Vule,	*to-morrow,*
T'vou,	*here,*
Vellu,	*there,*
P'lle,	*near,*
Allu mapu,	*afar off,*
Nau,	*under,* or *downwards,*
Huenu,	*above,*
Pule,	*againft,*
Allu pule,	*diftant,*
Chumgechi,	*on what manner,*
Vemgechi *or* vemge,	*on this manner,*

Mo, *or* meu, { the Latin prepofitions, *in, contra, cum, per, ob, propter, intra,*

Cay, and Chay, placed after a noun, *or, alone, and, perhaps,*
Huecu, *without.*

O o

To

(142)

To give some further idea of this language, I add the following specimens of it.

The SIGN of the CROSS.

Santa cruz ni gnelmeu, inchin in pu
By the sign of the holy cross, from our
caynemo montulmoin, Dios, inchin in
enemies deliver us, O GOD, our
Apo; Chao, Votch'm cay, Spiritu Santo cay,
Lord; the Father, and Son, and the Holy Ghost,
ni wimeu. Amen.
in the name of. Amen.

The Beginning of the LORD's PRAYER.

Inchin in Chao, huenumeuta m'leymi,
Our Father, in Heaven thou that art,
ufchingepe mi wi; eymi mi toquin.
hallowed be thy name; thy kingdom
inchinmo cupape; eymi mi piel,
to us may it come; thy will,
chumgechi vemgey huenu-mapumo,
as it is done in Heaven,
vemgechi cay vemengepe tue-mapumo; &c.
so likewise may it be done on earth; &c.

The Beginning of the CREED.

Mupiltun Dios, Chaomo vilpepilvoe, huenu
I believe in GOD, the Father Almighty, of Heaven
vemvoe, tue vemvoe cay; inchin in Apo
the maker, and of earth the maker also; in our Lord
Jesu Christomo cay, veyni m'ten Votch'm, &c.
JESUS CHRIST also, his only Son, &c.

[The

(143)

The Beginning of the Christian Doctrine.

Q. Chumten Dios m'ley? *How many Gods are there?*
 A. Quine m'ten.   *One only.*
 Q. Cheu m'ley ta Dios?   *Where is* GOD?
A. Huenu-mapumo, tue-mapumo, *In Heaven, in earth,*
vill-mapumo fume cay, *and in all the world wherefoever.*
 Q. Iney cam Dios?   *Who is* GOD?
A. Dios Chao, GOD *the Father,* Dios Votch'm, GOD *the Son,*
 Dios Spiritu Santo; cay quila Perfona geyum,
 GOD *the Holy Ghoft;* *and being three Perfons,*
 quiney Dios m'ten, *are one* GOD *only.*
Q. Chumgechi, quila Perfona geyum, quine m'ten ta Dios?
 How, being three Perfons,   GOD *is one alone?*
   A. Tvachi quila Perfona quine
   Thefe three Perfons have one only
 gen-n'gen, veyula quine m'ten ta Dios.
 Being, for this GOD *is one alone.*

Thefe fpecimens are accommodated to the Indian ex-
preffion, and intermixed with a few Spanifh words, where
the Indian idiom is infufficient, or might give a falfe idea.
And this, with the fhort vocabulary annexed, may fuffice to
give a fmall but imperfect notion of this language.

I omit feveral common words, becaufe they have been
already explained.

VOCABU-

(144)

VOCABULARY.

P'LLU, the foul, a spirit.
Lonco, the head, the hair.
Az, the face.
N'ge, the eyes.
Wun or Huun, the mouth.
Gehuun, the tongue.
Yu, the nose.
Voſo, the teeth, the bones.
Anca, the body.
Pue, the belly.
Cuugh, the hand.
Namon, the foot.
Pinque, the heart.
P'nen, a child.
Nahue, a daughter.
Peni, a brother.
Penihuen, own brothers.
Huinca, a Spaniard.
Seche, a neat Indian.
Huenuy, a friend.
Caynie, an enemy.
Huincha, a head-fillet.
Makun, a mantle.
Lancaitu, glaſs-beads.
Cofque, bread.
Ipe, food.
In, or ipen, to eat.
Ilo, fleſh.
Ilon, to eat fleſh.
Putun, drink, to drink.
Putumun, a cup.
Chilca, writing.
Chilcan, to write.
Sengu, a word, language; alſo a thing.
Huayqui, a lance.
Huayquitun, to lance.
Chinu, a knife, a ſword.
Chingoſcun, to wound.
Chingoſquen, to be wounded.
Conan, a ſoldier.
Conangean, he that is to be a ſoldier.
Amon, to walk or go.
Anun, to ſit.
Anupeum, a ſeat or ſtool.

Anumahuun, to feel inwardly.
Poyquelhuun, to feel, or perceive.
Con'n, to enter.
Tipan, to go out.
Cupaln, to bring.
Entun, to take away.
Aſeln, to be averſe.
Aſelgen, to hate.
M'len, to be, to poſſeſs.
Mongen, life, to live.
Mongetun, to revive.
Suam, the will.
Suamtun, to will.
Pepi, power.
Pepilan, to be able.
Quimn, knowledge, to know.
Quimeln, to learn.
Quimelcan, to teach.
Pangi, a lion.
Choique, an oſtrich.
Achahual, a cock or hen.
Malu, a large lizard or iguana.
Cuſa, a ſtone, an egg.
Saiguen, a flower.
Milya, gold.
Lien, ſilver.
Cullyin, money, payment.
Cullingen, to be rich.
Cunnubal, poor, miſerable, an orphan.
Cum panilhue (red metal) copper.
Choe panilhue (yellow metal) braſs.
Gepun, colour, or painting.
Saman, a trade, an artificer.
Mamel, a tree, wood.
Mamel-ſaman, a carpenter.
Suca-ſaman, a houſe-builder.
Antuigh, the ſun, a day.
Cuyem or Kiyem, the moon, a month.
Tipantu, a year.
K'tal, fire.
Aſee, hot.
Choſee, cold.
Atutuy, it is ſhivering cold.

THE END.

www.ingramcontent.com/pod-product-compliance
Lightning Source LLC
Chambersburg PA
CBHW030341170426
43202CB00010B/1203